Erik Castenskiold has devoted many years to helping people as they go through the deep pain of divorce and separation. His courses at HTB, which have grown and developed over time, have helped many, many people. This book is the fruit of all he has learned and offers love, support, and guidance to anyone in need.

NICKY GUMBEL

"Filled with compassion, empathy and wisdom… Erik gives real hope to those who have experienced a broken relationship."

NICKY AND SILA LEE

Restored Lives

Recovery from divorce and separation

Erik Castenskiold

MONARCH
BOOKS

Published by
Lion Hudson Limited
Wilkinson House, Jordan Hill Business Park,
Banbury Road, Oxford OX2 8DR, England
www.lionhudson.com

ISBN 978 0 85721 476 8
e-ISBN 978 0 85721 480 5

First edition 2013

Acknowledgments
Extract pp. 29–30 taken from *The Real Monty: The Autobiography of Colin
Montgomerie* by Colin Montgomerie and Lewine Mair, The Orion Publishing
Group, London. Copyright © 2002 Colin Montgomerie. Used with permission.
Extract pp. 105–107 taken from from *Rumours of Another World* by Philip
Yancey (Zondervan International, 2003, pp.223–224). Copyright © 2003 by
SCCT. Used by permission of Zondervan. www.zondervan.com

A catalogue record for this book is available from the British Library

Printed and bound in the UK, October 2020, LH57.

Contents

Foreword

Nicky and Sila Lee

Several years ago we met a young woman who had got married in her twenties. Two years later, her husband was having an affair and proceeded to divorce her. She was devastated. In addition, at a time when she was in acute need of support, she felt too ashamed to face the very people who would help her most at the church she was attending. Soon afterwards she was looking online and saw the Restored Lives course advertised on a church website. Before even attending the course her immediate response was, "That is a group who will understand what I am going through." She attended the course and, like hundreds of others before her and since, she found the support she needed to help her through the most painful experience of her life.

The advice she received from Erik Castenskiold, the leader of the course at our church, Holy Trinity Brompton, over many years, is now enshrined in this book and can help thousands of others in similar situations. Erik writes not just out of his own painful experience, but also from his long experience of helping many men and women to work through the devastation that separation and divorce cause. His writing, like his speaking, is filled with compassion, empathy, and wisdom. By refusing to avoid the hard choices of taking responsibility, and giving and receiving forgiveness, Erik gives real hope to those who have experienced a broken relationship.

"You may feel that you are sitting isolated in a small boat

in the midst of your own personal storm…" writes Erik. If you relate to that feeling, then read on. This book will help you for two reasons. First, it is not just theory. Erik offers time-tested practical tools that can be easily and quickly put into practice and that will make an immediate difference – tools for communicating better with an estranged partner and for resolving conflict more effectively; skills that will benefit every relationship now and in the years ahead.

The second reason is that the book is packed full of personal stories of others who have faced relationship breakdown. Their experiences will show you that you are not alone and you will learn from their insights and from what they have discovered. As Erik describes them: "The people in this book are normal, everyday people from all walks of life: different backgrounds, different break-ups, different families, different faiths, different levels of income, different hopes, different fears, and different expectations. But they all speak of the same end point – a restored life. These people are living testimonies to the knowledge that a full recovery can happen and that there *is* life after separation and divorce."

We have seen Erik doing everything he can to support marriages, while at the same time helping those who have experienced relationship breakdown. Some people who have attended Restored Lives have decided to have another go at saving their marriage and have subsequently done The Marriage Course, (a course designed to help couples strengthen their relationship). In other cases, as you will read, it has been the other way round. We have been so grateful to Erik and his team for running Restored Lives year after year so that as a church community we can both strengthen marriages and support those whose marriages have broken down.

Our hope and prayer for this book are not just that individuals will benefit from reading it, but that many people who want to help others will pick it up and be inspired to start running the Restored Lives course themselves. The resources are available through the Restored Lives website. And then we believe that you, like us, will hear story after story from grateful people, as together we reach out in the name of Jesus Christ to offer friendship, support, and hope.

Nicky and Sila Lee
Authors of *The Marriage Book* and *The Parenting Book*

Acknowledgments

This book would not be here if it had not been for the many people who walked this path with me. Their lives are the real proof that Restored Lives are possible, and that is where I have found my inspiration. The full list is too long, but I would especially like to thank the following people who have made the stories, guided the wisdom, and encouraged me to continue:

Christopher Compston
Miles and Deborah Protter
Helen Adam
Carol Rawlence
Weng Lee
Angie Wilkie
Kate Meadows
Peter Detre
Greg Love
John Figuredo
Sandy Millar
Nicky Gumbel

Nicky and Sila Lee
Marilyn Heward-Mills
Willem Kok
Helen Jennings
Thomas Martin
Kathy Miller
Matthew Bates
Kay and Robin Lawrence
Cathy and Patrick Butcher
Jules, Luke, Hannah, and Daniel

In this book a number of stories are told of people who have attended the Restored Lives course. In relationship breakdown there are often two different sides to the same story, and someone else close to the situation may view things differently. As a result, I have sought to be respectful of both parties and to present the facts neutrally, while focusing on the journey of the storyteller. In addition, all names and key identifying features have been changed to preserve anonymity.

Introduction

Relationship breakdown will affect all of us at some stage in life. For some people it will be second-hand through a friend or family member, but others will experience it first hand. Many speak of it as the biggest crisis they have ever faced.

Even though it is so common, it's a sad truth that most people feel incredibly isolated and lonely as they go on this journey. This book is designed to break through that isolation and come alongside you to give you the tools, skills, and encouragement that you need to move on successfully from your relationship breakdown.

The problems and challenges that arise in relationship breakdown can be difficult and complex. There are no prizes for going through this process all by yourself. I would therefore strongly encourage you to have someone to talk to as you go through this experience. This book can act as a guide but, with challenges sometimes arising on a daily basis, having a trusted friend by your side to listen and encourage you in the right direction can also be vital.

I have seen this lifeline in action time after time on the Restored Lives course, where people come from many different backgrounds and meet others who are experiencing serious relationship breakdown. While friends and family may misunderstand your emotions, those whom you meet on the Restored Lives course will have similar thoughts, feelings, complaints, hopes, fears, and questions. Hearing people's stories will make you feel more normal and their experience will help you to move forward. You will soon realize that your own experience can also help others, and this can be very rewarding.

The journey of recovery from relationship breakdown will take time, depending on your particular situation. For some people this book will be a useful checklist marking out the road map for recovery, while for others it may become a detailed guide to refer to when you get stuck on a particular matter. The book is a practical guide with a number of personal exercises – so get your pen out to note down your thoughts in this book or in a separate notebook, as this will help you to quickly crystallize the next steps.

The exciting pattern that we see on the Restored Lives course is watching a person experience radical change over a short period of time. Sometimes there is suddenly a deep understanding and clarity when previously there has been confusion. At other times it is the freedom that comes from letting go, or simply a confidence that there really is hope for the future. Whatever the reason, the end result is a transformed heart and mind, which can often be visible in the faces of those who attend, in the form of laughter and peace.

Whether your recovery takes a long time or a short time, whether you are recently divorced or have been struggling with a relationship breakdown for many years, you can successfully move on now. The experience of many, many people, often in incredibly difficult circumstances, is that the tools and skills discussed in this book are an effective means of recovery. It is an honour for me to come alongside you on your journey, and I hope and pray that you will soon have a restored and fulfilling life.

PART ONE

FACING THE EFFECTS OF WHAT'S HAPPENED

Chapter 1

There is hope

"I feel like a different woman… I know I'm not entirely there yet, but I also know it's a process, which can't be sidestepped or avoided. You have to embrace it as a horrid opportunity that, with God's grace, will enable you to grow and become a much better person."

Martha

Growing stronger from your break-up

Relationship breakdown is one of the most serious crises that anyone can face in life. The impact of separation and divorce is so significant that people can easily become submerged in a nightmare that makes it difficult for them to think past today, let alone plan for tomorrow. Life will be changing so much that they will be unsure of what to do next and how to do it. They will be thinking, "What will help me to move on successfully? Has anyone done this before?"

Yes, they have! It is possible to get rid of the pain and hurt, minimize the damage, and actually grow stronger as a person after a break-up. It's not a journey that anyone wants to take, nor is it an easy path, but there is a real possibility of a fulfilled, pain-free, restored life in the future. That has been my experience, and that of thousands of other people who have been through the same problems.

This hope is real, not because of the passage of time or the chance of winning a good financial settlement, but as a result of some practical tools that can help people at each stage of their journey. These tools have been forged by experts and professionals and purified in the furnace of first-hand experience of tragic relationship breakdowns. You will meet some of these people as we go through this book, and their stories speak loudly of the hope that exists for a better future.

This is my story:

When I married Karen, we were both full of confidence that our marriage would be a lifelong commitment and a success. We were happily married for four and a half years and had dated for four years before that, so we knew each other well. We had many joint interests and social activities and we had similar values and beliefs. Our friends called us the "cuddly couple" because we were always close and affectionate with each other and we never argued. We even started talking with friends about finding ways to help other couples to support their marriages. So it came as a huge surprise when Karen turned to me in bed one Saturday morning and told me she was having an affair.

I can still remember so much of that moment even though it was a long time ago now. It was a beautiful spring morning and the sun was shining in through the windows. I remember the smell of the room that we were staying in at the time. I recall the strangely cold way in which she started the conversation: "I want to tell you..." I found out later that events had forced her to tell me.

My world fell apart at that moment. As she told me that she was having an affair with a man at work, my heart was ripped out. The person to whom I had given my life, with whom I had entwined my whole being, tore me to shreds with those few words.

Over the next few days I tried to keep our marriage together and, initially, I thought that Karen would want to make our relationship work again – wasn't that what we had signed up for? But I soon realized that she was trying to continue her other relationship. This was not simply a one-off; it had been going on for six months without me or any of our friends knowing. I had to start working out what had gone wrong six or nine months before. What was it that I had missed? Where did I go wrong? Was I that stupid? I felt so lonely and broken.

It was a complicated affair. The man involved – Tim – was a friend from work whom Karen had brought to our home and introduced to me. He was actually engaged, and it was his fiancée who found Tim and Karen together at his house. The affair was out, which was why Karen had to tell me about it.

I remember the horror of that time as there was so much pain in the day-to-day events: piecing together what was going on, waiting to hear from Karen, trying to concentrate at work, finding a place to live, dealing with abusive phone calls from friends and relatives, talking to friends who didn't understand, trying to find something else to think about, the aimless daydreaming, separating possessions, sorting out finances, avoiding some people, feeling like an alien in a normal environment, hating social gatherings but being desperately lonely – there were so many painful things to deal with.

There was also a constant reassessment of the past, seeing it in a new light: for instance the time I had spent with Tim. I had made the effort to get to know him because he was "an important friend" to Karen and he seemed to want to spend time with me as well. I had played pool with him on various evenings and had even spent a night watching cricket with him, as he was an avid supporter. Why on earth had Tim and Karen wanted me to do this? Did it help their affair?

I remember the lies and deception over those six months. When she said that she wanted to study for her exams with Tim, I helped her to make time for it. Looking back, was it just so that she could spend time with him? To me it felt as if her life was now one whole structure of lies, one lie supporting another. I moved out of our home and initially went from house to house. I couldn't sleep, I drank too much, and I was restless – I would often walk around the streets of London, late at night (not the smartest thing to do). I felt lost in heart and mind.

In the end, Karen didn't get together with Tim, but neither did she want to get back together with me. It was the worst time of my life. I had shared my life, my intimacy, and my dreams with her; I had given her all my trust, and it seemed so easily thrown away.

I began to put my life back together and things got better. I relied heavily on friends who could guide me through the difficult decisions that I had to make and encourage me when life was very black. I went on the Recovery from Separation and Divorce Course (now retitled Restored Lives), where I met other people in the same situation as me, and I started making proactive choices that helped me to move on.

The acid test is that I can now look back at all the events that took place concerning my relationship breakdown without feeling the pain and hurt that were so inextricably linked to those events. I have no fear of bumping into Karen or her new family and can talk about that time without shame, regret, or anger.

Importantly, the break-up is now a positive influence on my relationships, enabling me to have closer, deeper, and more meaningful relationships with friends and family.

Tools to help you recover

My experience is not an isolated one. There are many people who have not just been able to survive their relationship breakdown but to grow stronger through it. While running Restored Lives over the last ten years, I have seen over a thousand people work through the biggest crisis of their life.

Some have children; some do not. Some were married for many years; others were cohabiting for a short time. Some have been divorced for a long time; others have just separated. Some have made the difficult decision to initiate separation; others have had it forced upon them. What unites them all are the choices and problems that they have had to face and the tools that have helped them recover.

I have seen faces and lives transformed in what is sometimes a remarkably short time. For some people it can take longer, especially if they have children and an acrimonious relationship with their partner. However, Restored Lives highlights the path and the tools that will accelerate your recovery.

It is important to note at the outset that **time is not the healer**, it's the choices we make. Time certainly lessens the intensity of feelings and provides you with new opportunities and distractions, but it does not heal the underlying problems that remain inside our hearts and minds. I have seen people who are still suffering from the pain and hurt caused by a relationship breakdown many years after the event. What heals the underlying issues are the **choices** that you make that enable you to move on successfully, and the good news is that these are in your control.

The journey of recovery

It is useful to picture and understand the overall journey of relationship breakdown so that you can see where you are now and where you are going. This diagram charts your emotional well-being as time goes by.

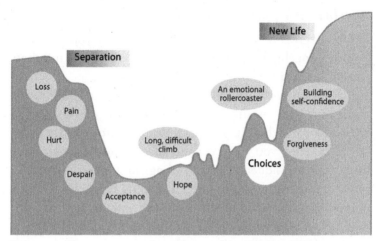

We typically start at a relatively good level of well-being, but then, when cracks begin to appear in our relationship, we quickly fall into the valley of despair with all its associated feelings of loss, pain, and hurt.

At the bottom of the valley there are seeds of acceptance and hope, which start to lift us slowly and gradually upwards. Our journey of recovery will have many ups and downs but the long difficult climb will be made easier by the choices we make. For me, letting go of the pain and embracing forgiveness were very important parts of my recovery.

It is vitally important to know that we can finish our journey at a higher level of emotional well-being than we had before we were separated.

Personal exercise

Where are you now on the journey? Mark it on the diagram.
Where do you think your ex-partner is on the journey? Mark this on the diagram too.

Tools to enable you to recover

This book gives you the practical tools to enable you to recover from relationship breakdown. They are the keys to a fulfilling, pain-free, rewarding future.

To begin with, we will look at the issues relating to the downward part of the journey – the pain of relationship breakdown and the many feelings that arise from it. These can be difficult for you to face, especially if you have run away from them or hidden the bad feelings in a locked emotional box. Although it is challenging, don't skip this stage, because pinpointing the underlying reason for your pain is the first stage in permanently dealing with it and releasing the rest of your life from its effects.

The rest of the book is all about the upward part of your journey and the choices that you can make to accelerate your recovery. Two fundamental skills stand out: communication and letting go. Communication skills are at the heart of all relationships and are a key tool for helping you build your own confidence as well as improving your discussions with your ex. Letting go of the pain and the hurt in your life is hard, but central to moving on. We will highlight some practical steps to enable you to do this.

Personal exercise

What do you most need in your journey through relationship breakdown?

You may feel isolated and alone at the moment, overwhelmed by the storm that is encircling you, but you are not alone. Many other people have been through what you are going through, and now have restored lives. I will be using their stories and experiences to give you a light for your path through the storm.

Here is one from Martha.

Martha

My husband and I got on terribly well and we had a lot of happy times together. We were hugely compatible intellectually and we had lots and lots of interests in common. We were emotionally very different, but even so we married and had two children.

The real differences between us became profound when our daughter was two and a half and our son was three months old. I was diagnosed with an aggressive type of cancer and my husband and I dealt with this deeply traumatic situation in very different ways. For both of us it was extremely difficult, as neither of us knew whether I would live long enough to see the children grow up.

I know I did very little to support my husband during this time, but I was incredibly ill and had so much to deal with just for myself. It seemed to me that he coped with my cancer by completely retreating into his shell and taking a deliberate, conscious decision to let me deal with the whole thing by myself. He rarely came to the hospital, apart from the time when we met the oncologist to find out what my chances were of surviving. He didn't come to any of my chemotherapy or radiotherapy sessions, and I found this lack of involvement and support terribly difficult. I had some help with the children during the day, but during the nights and at weekends I was left to look after the children on my own, as my husband felt his job was too demanding to have his sleep and leisure time interrupted.

It was a truly terrible time for us as a family, and we both felt very unloved and neglected. Unfortunately, my husband happened to meet up with an old girlfriend not long afterwards, and they began an affair. This lasted for about two years, until I found out about it from his mobile phone, which was devastating.

I had been through so much trauma with my illness, and this new betrayal meant I really wanted to pack it in and boot him out. I felt, however, that we had to try to stay together as a family. I felt that, in order to face the children when they were older, I had to be able to say that I had tried everything I could to see whether there was anything in our marriage worth salvaging.

We tried some counselling but he wasn't very keen on that idea, as he felt he didn't have any problems to deal with. He said that I could go and have therapy if I wanted to, but it wasn't for him.

Just when I thought things couldn't get any worse, my husband started another relationship with someone I regarded as a very good friend. She was the mother of our son's best friend at school and I knew her extremely well – we'd even been away on holiday together.

I couldn't avoid her as we would see each other regularly at school; the boys were in the same class and were in the same cricket, football, and rugby teams. My children were only nine and eleven and this was a terribly difficult situation for them. In a heartbeat, it seemed that he had instantly and completely moved on. For three days a week he would live with us and then he'd be with this other woman for the rest of the week, which was extremely upsetting and confusing in equal measure.

How did you move on?

I did Restored Lives about four years ago and have come back as a helper on the course. I wish I'd known about it earlier on in my separation. When I came I was already divorced, but still overwhelmed with pain and grief – feeling I was caught in a black hole from which I couldn't climb out. I loved it for many reasons: I felt the practical advice was so helpful and I also drew a huge amount of support from hearing about other people's experiences. As recovery is a process, every time I listen to the talks I usually hear something new as I reach a different place in my journey to freedom.

The whole question of forgiveness was a big thing for me. I felt I had so much for which I had to forgive my ex. But I think the turning point was an enlightened piece of therapy which helped me to realize that I too had had a significant part to play in the collapse of our marriage. I realized that I could do nothing to change my ex. Every week I would shout about why he continued to make the choices he did – couldn't he see how much he was hurting the children and me? My therapist asked me: if my ex were blind, would I be angry that he couldn't see? This was a real moment of clarity for me and helped me at last to reach that point where I had to accept my ex as he was.

My children also had some very good therapy, which has changed their lives beyond belief. It's so easy to spout platitudes about children being resilient and coping terribly well with change; claiming that as long as they're not talking about the divorce or displaying any behavioural difficulties, then they must be "fine". But underneath it all they may be a seething mass of emotions, including anger, resentment, confusion, and a profound sense of loss. I think that unless children are given the opportunity to discuss, process, and accept these emotions very early on, they will take them through into adulthood, which will in turn affect their future relationships.

How do you feel now?

I feel like a different woman. I feel utterly transformed and, quite remarkably, I can even wish my ex well in his new life. I never, ever, thought I'd be able to stand in front of a roomful of strangers and speak about some of the worst aspects of my life without breaking down. I know I'm not entirely there yet, but I also know it's a process, which can't be sidestepped or avoided. You have to embrace it as a horrid opportunity that, with God's grace, will enable you to grow and become a much better person.

TOOLBOX TO TAKE AWAY
There is hope

Hold on to hope – many people have recovered and feel stronger now

See where you are in the journey – even through ups and downs, you're moving forward in your path ahead

Recognize where your ex is on the journey – they will often be at a different stage

The choices that you make will enable you to move on successfully

There is a path through your storm

Chapter 2

Understanding the emotional impact

"I remember the… big list of feelings and emotions. I felt all those things, every one of them, and I just sat and cried for the whole evening. I just couldn't believe the pain I was in. Every time someone spoke I began to cry again. I was very depressed, sad, broken…

"I'm stronger now and think I'm pretty close to the high point of the journey of recovery. It feels good."

Karina

What can we change?

We cannot change the past and we cannot change our ex, but we *can* change ourselves, and that *will* affect our future.

As we look at the impact of relationship breakdown on our life we need to recognize the things we can and can't change. We cannot change the past; it's happened. Many people have tried to alter their ex, but it rarely works! What we can control is our attitude, our outlook, and our own activities, all of which *will* have a big impact on what subsequently happens to us.

This is the best starting point as we look at the pain of the past and begin to choose whether this will continue to harm us in the future.

The impact of relationship breakdown

A few people find that their relationship breakdown is relatively easy and the emotional impact is small. However, many people find themselves consumed by the pain of separation and divorce. It hurt me desperately and I know that, whatever your circumstances, there will be pain and hurt. We have to acknowledge this before we can move on. It hurts us and it hurts others around us as well. The good news is that there *are* ways of dealing successfully with this pain.

> I have a lot of experience of pain. As well as being once married to a doctor, I have had numerous sporting injuries. I have broken a finger, a thumb, a toe, my arm, and a couple of ribs. I have cracked my knee cap and had three other knee operations. A while ago, I snapped my left Achilles tendon. Then, four years later, I snapped my right one.
>
> The first time I snapped an Achilles I didn't know what had happened. I was on the playing field and it felt as if someone behind me had kicked me very hard on the back of the leg. I turned round to tell the person a few core facts of life, but there was no one there. I hopped off the pitch and went to hospital. I saw a nurse who poked at my leg, and it was agony. Then I saw a junior doctor and a senior registrar, who both pressed my leg and, again, it was agony. Finally, the surgeon inspected my leg and, yes, more agony, but at least he was able to say that he could fix my tendon by stitching it back together.

What I took from this was the understanding that the doctor needs to know *where* the pain is before they can give the right diagnosis and start to treat the problem.

In the same way, we need to understand where our emotional pain is so that we can start to relieve it. Just like a doctor, we need to develop an awareness of exactly where our pain comes from, so that we can start to deal with it.

The grief of relationship breakdown

When a relationship ends, the emotional impact is enormous. For some, it brings a huge sense of relief, but many of us feel guilt and shame as well as a profound sense of loss. In some ways it can feel worse than losing someone through death, when all your friends and family will gather round you and support you through your grieving process. One woman whose partner left her said this:

> If he had died, I would have known that he hadn't wanted to leave, and I could have concentrated on coming to terms with never seeing him again. But, as it was, I knew he had wanted to get away from me. Added to that, I kept on bumping into him and his new girlfriend, which was torture.

Judge Christopher Compston, who started the Recovery from Divorce and Separation course in the early 1990s, says that the pain of his divorce was worse than the trauma of his son's death:

> I was devastated when my son Joshua died. It was a tragic death. He was a hugely talented and charismatic art entrepreneur. He was only twenty-five, and a maverick, but we had a close relationship.
>
> The circumstances of his death were unusual. He had found some anaesthetic thrown away in a skip and we will never know whether he died from a freak accident or suicide. It was also a very public death, with obituaries in the national newspapers, as he was a rising star with close connections with Damien Hirst and Tracey Emin.
>
> We received immense and comforting support from so many different people. In addition I had the distraction of four other children who needed my time and focus to help them overcome their loss.

Divorce is different. Your partner, who has been your closest
support, is lost. People give you muted sympathy and many people
don't know how to help. Some friends ignore your loss and tell you,
"Don't worry – you'll get over it."

The losses involved in relationship breakdown

We have not just lost our partner – we have sustained a series
of related losses. We have lost our role as part of a couple.
We may have lost daily habits and routines. We have lost the
security of having someone by our side and the comfort of
having someone with whom to share life's ups and downs. We
may have lost our home and financial security – the financial
impact of divorce is often huge. Maybe we have lost our
dreams or our vision for the future. If we have children, we
may have lost daily contact with them. If they live with us,
then we may miss having the other parent there to help. We
may also feel a loss of self-esteem and a loss of our place in our
social network. Even if the separation has taken place by our
choice, and ultimately for the good, there is still the loss of
what might have been.

For many of us, this loss is constantly with us, causing us
to limp around with the pain of relationship breakdown. We
need this pain to become like an alarm bell that helps us to
pinpoint the thing that needs to be sorted and healed. It's no
good just ignoring it or sticking a plaster on it. The point is
that pain, whether physical or emotional, demands action to
relieve it.

You may ask, "Why think about my painful feelings?
Why bring them up when they hurt so much and it happened
so long ago?" The problem with pain is that if we carry it
inside us, however well hidden, it will act like a landmine.
Any unexpected trigger will cause an explosion, whether in

outbursts of anger, being overwhelmed by depression, or in running away from a situation or event. It's also bad for our physical health.

Emotional roller coaster

Many of us know that, especially in the early stages of relationship breakdown, we can quickly turn from a normal, interesting person into a confused bag of emotions; we don't know whether we're coming or going. I can assure you that this downward cycle is only temporary.

This confused emotional state is described well by Colin Montgomerie, one of the world's best golfers. He was married to Eimear for sixteen years and they have three children. In his autobiography, after the couple initially separated, he said this:

She snapped. Eyeing me with a cold contempt, she announced that she had finally had enough. Golf, she pronounced, had taken over my life to the point where I would do better on my own. The marriage might as well be over. In fact, it was over in her eyes.

I knew at once that this was serious. But my overriding feeling was one of fury. Half of me wanted to scream at her. Instead of retaliating, I put my head down and walked into the night. Although at that stage I was feeling wronged and self-righteous, I thought fleetingly of how I would feel if Eimear were not there for me.

To say that I was shattered is an understatement. I felt that everything I had done, everything I had achieved just fell through the floor. I cried a lot – it was a bad, bad time. I felt a failure, immediately. And I felt that my whole life had just come to a complete grinding halt.

I started tramping the streets of London. I spent a month in a hotel in which I left the hotel at about 10 pm each night and would return, foot-weary and heavy-hearted, at three in the morning or even later. Sometimes people would look at me with recognition in their faces, but then they would think again. It couldn't be Colin Montgomerie, the golfer, walking the streets at this hour of the night. I was disturbed at the sight of regular families. Every time I saw one I felt like going up to them and saying, "Do you realize how lucky you are?"

Colin Montgomerie and Lewine Mair, *The Real Monty: The Autobiography of Colin Montgomerie*

Feelings and emotions

This description gives a strong sense of the powerful emotions provoked by separation and the paralysing sense of confusion and "blur". Many of us can relate to aspects of Colin's experience. Equally, our feelings may be very different from his. Obviously, our emotions will be different depending on what stage of the journey we are at. However, it is vital to spend some time recognizing exactly what we are thinking and feeling, right now.

Personal exercise

What are you feeling? Write down the emotions you are feeling about your relationship breakdown. Write down what you regularly think about at the moment.

On Restored Lives we give people the opportunity to say what they are feeling and this is the list of feelings and emotions that came from one evening:

Anger, shame, loneliness, regret, fear, revenge, loss, shock, alcoholic tendencies, bad-tempered, antagonistic, not focused, like a fraud, suicidal, selfish, bitter, nomadic, frustrated, grieving, bereft, in limbo, determined to cause pain, unwanted, disappointed, scared, disbelief, untrusting, cynical, committed, annoyed, fragile, another statistic, mourning, confusion, lost, betrayed, guilty, alone, sadness, hopeful, dejection, abandoned, failure, used, misunderstood, helpless, vengeful, anxious, restless, murderous, depressed, free, lighter, relief, second chance, happy, excited, good riddance, own time, own money, tired, childish, unkindest cut, recovered, refocused, peaceful, centred, re-energized, rediscovery, sexually frustrated, too many choices, isolated, responsible, cheated, distracted, matronly, overwhelmed, disorientated, regretful, very cheesed off, poorer, wasted time, devastated for children, tearful, labelled, sleepless, lack of confidence, aggressive.

This is a huge range of emotions and shows the extent of what people go through, positive and negative. Many individuals feel that they relate to nearly all of these emotions at different times.

The process of dealing with pain

I want to assure you that there are ways of dealing with these feelings successfully. You don't have to bury pain or hide it away; you can be free from it.

The door to recovery is opened by understanding your thoughts and feelings. Then you need to pinpoint the underlying reason for the painful issue or emotional trigger, which then, with the right tools in your hand, enables you to choose how to resolve it and to tackle the problem proactively.

Knowing your feelings

Some people find it easy to express what they feel. However, many find it quite difficult either to verbalize or even to know what they are feeling. This skill can be learned – I've done it.

I was brought up in a family and an environment that did not express feelings. It was only after my divorce that I realized that this was a problem and was holding me back.

I can't remember a single argument with Karen, which I thought was a good sign – but it was not. I didn't express my feelings because I was not used to doing it and did not want conflict. All I did was ignore the feelings or bottle them up. However, my feelings would inevitably come out in one way or another, either through my being overly silent, making unkind comments, or sometimes exploding days later. Not being able to express feelings was unhealthy for our marriage and for me.

I knew that I had to get over this problem and learn to express my feelings better. So, with the help of a close friend, I promised to say something straight away if we were together and I felt anything negative (even if it was just "Ouch" or "That was unkind"). In this safe environment we could then ask a number of questions: what was I really feeling?; what was the trigger?; why did I feel like that?; and what could be done about it? The important thing was to mention it as soon as I felt something inside me reacting or my temperature rising.

I found out that there were four reasons for my slow response:

- not recognizing the emotion;
- not realizing that saying something would help me;
- not knowing how to express what I was feeling;
- a fear of saying something unkind or unhelpful.

Being in touch with what you are feeling will enable you to move on more quickly. It will empower you to pinpoint the key issue that may be holding you back and is a vital part of the recovery process, as well as a core skill for any relationship.

If you found it difficult to write down your own emotions then it is helpful to spend some more time thinking about them. Use the list of words earlier in this chapter and read through them a couple of times to see which ones you respond to most.

Personal exercise

During the day, write down any feelings or any strong thoughts as soon as they occur. Then think about what caused them. This will enable you to recognize your feelings and their triggers.

What's driving those emotions?

It is vital to look behind your emotions to see what is generating them. Often when going through a relationship breakdown we find that some feelings such as frustration, anger, or depression come back regularly. However, these emotions can arise as a result of something else, such as fear, which is why they are sometimes referred to as "secondary emotions".

Two stories bring these feelings to life and can help us start to unpack what is driving these emotions and what we can do about them. Both stories are from parents with three teenage children, the first from Annie and the second from Roger.

Annie

The most difficult part for me was recognizing my feelings. My overriding awareness was of being hurt, but I also felt self-pity, hatred, isolation, uselessness, and hopelessness — and most of the others you can think of too!

So why was it that, when I bumped into someone in the supermarket and they asked me how I was, I would say, "Oh, I'm fine!"? (I now think that "fine" stands for Fearful Insecure Negative and Emotional!) I can see now that in the early weeks and months after my separation I teetered on the edge of a mental breakdown. I am a "coper" and a "doer", but slowly I slipped into a sort of parallel universe where everything was strange – I lived in the same house, with the same school run, the same supermarket, and the same neighbours, but my whole existence was totally altered. It still looked the same, but I had lost my husband somewhere along the way.

In fact, looking the same was really hard because I wanted people to see that my life was now completely different. One very bleak night I went into the kitchen to cut myself. I had heard of self-harm – it's what troubled teenagers do, not forty-something mothers – but the pain was so intense on the inside that I wanted to see some sign of it on the outside. Those feelings really shocked me.

During those early days I spent most of my time in the garden talking to my brother's wife on the phone, with a glass of wine and a packet of cigarettes at hand (I had not smoked for sixteen years). Sometimes she would answer my call and I would be unable even to speak. She would just say, "Oh, Annie, is that you?" and start talking to me. She was my lifeline.

For me, the beginning of the process of recovery was acceptance and that took a long time. My husband of fifteen years had left and was living with another woman and her three children. I told myself it was a phase, a mid-life crisis; he would come to his senses, and what a great personal story it would be to discuss with my friends! Hello?!? What planet was I living on? Planet Unreality. My friends could see so much more clearly than I could that it was over, but I clung to hope – every phone call, every text message, every email meant the possibility of getting back together.

So, for me, acceptance of the finality of my position was a breakthrough. The next step was realizing that I had reactive depression – if you are a coper and doer by instinct, this comes as a huge shock! My daughter, then aged about nine, said one day on the way to school, "Please don't come into the school if you are going to start crying again." This was a big sign that I was not OK and I went to see my GP, who put me on antidepressants as well as helping me to obtain a lot of supervision and counselling. The antidepressants seriously changed my life – I had slid into a deep pit so slowly that I had not really noticed. The difference was fantastic! I could function again, make small decisions, make plans, and think. I started making good choices and I stopped crying every day.

I was on antidepressants for nearly two years, but am off them now. For me they meant survival. I know that there is a lot of embarrassment about taking them, but I now tell everyone who will stand still for long enough, "If you had diabetes you would take insulin, so what's the difference?"

Another breakthrough for me was recognizing how angry I was! A friend suggested I go to see an anger counsellor and I said, "I am not angry!" I was so wrong. The counsellor got me to look at years of resentment and anger that I had stored up and that really helped me to let them go.

People generally do one of two things when they are angry: they either internalize their rage and do nothing, or they throw plates and scream. I did both! The problem with internalizing anger is that it does our bodies a lot of damage and then we "leak" anger, which in my case involved being very critical, making snide comments, and being resentful. I was brought up to believe that I should not show anger. That makes life very confusing when you inevitably do get angry, because you have no idea what to do with it. Now, when my daughter gets angry, I applaud her (in an appropriate way) because she tells me how it really feels.

What I have learned about anger is how very destructive it can be in a relationship. The first stage was to recognize that I was angry, to acknowledge how that felt, to try to work out what was making me angry (sounds easier than it is), and then to let it out in a constructive way. For me, that would usually be by talking to a *trusted friend, writing about it (and hiding the book), and banging pillows with a baseball bat. If anger is an ongoing problem in your life, do seek professional help. Leaking anger, like a dripping tap, can cause a huge amount of damage.*

The other thing that really helped me was doing some part-time work. I had not worked outside the home since the children were small, and I found making a tiny bit of money for myself very empowering and good for my self-esteem. It's also good to try to be sociable. That is really hard when you are depressed, because you tend to feel grim and you can't enjoy what everyone else thinks is fun. So try to spend time with people who will be gentle with you and do non-threatening things, like going to the cinema.

Roger

I was shocked when I heard that my ex wanted a divorce and wanted me to leave the family home. The loss of daily contact with my children, my own flesh and blood, was the most painful thing. This was then coupled with the loss of a nice family home and moving to numerous bedsits, which sadly cost me as much as the mortgage on my house. I had to keep moving from one rented or temporary accommodation to another and over a three-year period I had around twelve different addresses. It was very depressing and I had suicidal thoughts. I was not sleeping well, surviving on just three or four hours' sleep.

There was so much that I had taken for granted. I found it very difficult to accept that my ex was now involved with someone else especially as the relationship was with another female. I was brought up in a very traditional Catholic family where there was no history of divorce at all, which made things very hard for me to understand and come to terms with.

This period was made even bleaker when I lost my job and my father died. My self-esteem was at rock bottom. The pain was exacerbated by my ex initially denying me contact with the children.

This was made worse still because I didn't have a comfortable home that they could come to, which invariably meant taking them out when I saw them, and having to spend money that was in very short supply.

The loss of simple daily family life had a really negative impact on me. Things got so bad that I almost moved into a rehabilitation scheme run by the local authority, but fortunately a very good friend from church and his family took me in for six months. Daily contact with this family was in many ways part of my recovery.

One of the best bits of advice I was given was to keep busy and develop a new social life. I did not have much money so I joined a walking club; we went out all day and I could talk to a few others who had also gone through relationship breakdowns. I volunteered to help with various charities and on courses such as Restored Lives. Not only did I get social contact there but I could see others who were in a worse plight than I was and paradoxically this was in itself healing.

I also started doing a lot more exercise, as I found it helped lift me out of my depression and mood swings.

These stories highlight a number of emotions that you may be feeling:

ANGER

Anger may arise in your life simply because of the major upheaval that you are going through and all the changes you are experiencing. At other times anger can be generated by fear: fear of losing your marriage; fear of being alone; fear of losing your social network; or fear of not being with your children again. Knowing and acknowledging your fears is an important step in starting to overcome them.

We also need to be aware of the way in which we react to our children's anger, which may not be helpful either – we may get cross with children just because they too are angry, or say "Don't be angry".

Anger is a dangerous emotion that can affect many other parts of our lives and, as adults, we often develop a number of ways of hiding or releasing our anger without knowing it. Both adults and children need to understand the underlying causes of their anger and find positive ways of dealing with it. Here are some useful steps you can take to deal with it, whatever your age:

- Pinpoint the trigger of your anger – what "makes your blood boil"?

- Pause and count to ten – it will prevent you from saying something that you may regret and help you to think straight. Taking time out to cool down may be good for everyone.

- Understand the underlying cause of this anger – e.g. change, fear, resentment, etc. Once you have identified the specific underlying cause, you can begin to think of ways of dealing with it.

- Express your anger assertively, not aggressively – make it clear what the issue is. Don't be demanding, pushy, or disrespectful.

- Convert or redirect your anger – it can be dissipated in a different direction. Doing something physical is good; talking to someone can be very helpful; doing something creative such as drawing, writing, or singing is helpful; or some form of relaxation to rid yourself of the anger inside you can be beneficial.

GUILT

We feel guilty when we regret something that we have done, either in the light of our own expectations or when viewed against someone else's expectations. Relationships are complex and there will always be aspects in which we could have been a better partner. When a relationship breaks up there will often be feelings of guilt.

It is important to recognize that there are circumstances in which guilt is appropriate, for example if we promise to meet someone somewhere and then choose not to without letting them know. However, there are circumstances where guilt is misplaced, for instance when a child feels responsible for his or her parents' divorce.

No one is perfect, and if we are concerned about the impact of our actions on others then guilt will be an issue we need to deal with. Because wedding vows include the expectation of marriage being permanent, divorce is itself often something that we can feel guilty about.

Taking these steps can enable you to move on:

- Admit to yourself the specific matters that you feel guilty about, rather than just having a generally guilty conscience.

- Write them down or talk them through with a friend, as openness helps to clarify the issue honestly.

- Check for wrong guilt. Think about whether your expectations of the right outcome were reasonable.

- Where you can, say sorry and try to make amends.

- Forgive yourself and let go.

It is important to deal with guilt and later we will be looking in much more detail at the tools that can help you to do this successfully.

SHAME

Guilt and shame are often confused, but it is vital to see the difference between the two because shame can cause deeper, long-term problems.

Guilt is connected with an external event or an action that has caused pain, for example that our relationship broke down. Shame relates to how we feel about ourselves and how we believe other people see us. It is this internalization of an event that makes shame much more dangerous, because it is now not about the event but about ourselves and who we are – we are faulty, worthless, or not good enough.

In cases of guilt there is often an obvious action or potential remedy available, such as to apologize and make amends. But with shame, because it relates to how we think of ourselves, we need to understand the situation in a different light or from a different perspective so that these feelings can be endured, absorbed, minimized, or denied.

There are instances in which shame can be positive. Shame stops us from walking down the street naked, and sometimes we speak of "shaming people into a right response", for example to stop racism.

But, more often, shame can be toxic, stopping you from treating yourself properly. It can inhibit close relationships and can be highly destructive.

Shame can arise from various circumstances but it is often formed by the way your parents and family have treated you. A person who has lived in a very controlling, neglectful, or abusive family will often carry what is nowadays referred to as "toxic" shame.

Shame can also be contagious. People filled with shame can often be controlling, rigid perfectionists, and they can (to protect themselves) project their own shame onto someone else.

We therefore need to be aware of the underlying symptoms of internal inadequacies that can highlight shame in action.

Sadly, merely going through separation and divorce can itself create toxic shame for many people. Sometimes communities create an automatic distance around people who are getting divorced. At other times our friends and family react in a way that increases our feelings of shame. We move from seeing divorce as a horrendous event to believing that we are deficient and defective.

The consequences of shame are widespread and destructive. They range from anger, envy, and anxiety through to sadness, loneliness, and depression. Shame also increases the desire for secrecy and hiding your feelings – you will say to yourself, "Why highlight them when everyone will say I'm wrong?" As a result of this, it is important to recognize shame when it arises and to know the steps to help you deal with it.

These are the important actions to focus on:

- Confront the cause of your shame. Try to be specific and if necessary write down a list of things that make you feel deficient in other people's eyes. What exactly is making you feel not good enough?

- Separate the external events that have happened from the feelings of shame and lack of worth. This is the key to understanding the misconceptions that are driving your feelings of shame. For example, "My family is angry that I am separating" causes shame that is tempered with the fact that "I have to protect myself from an abusive partner". Isolate the unhelpful views of other people that are causing you pain.

- Talk with someone about these emotions. It is vital to discuss them with someone you trust.

- Joining a support group is amazingly helpful, and I have seen many people come to a group and recognize that many kind, intelligent, attractive, normal people go through divorce – you are not a one-off!

- Build your confidence in other areas. Do something you enjoy or know you are good at – it will build your confidence that you are good enough.

- Acceptance: understand the difference between what you can change and what you can't. Deal with any guilt and then accept your situation.

- Forgive and let go. We need to forgive ourselves and forgive others for the pain and shame that they have laid on us. We discuss forgiveness and letting go in detail in Part Three.

DEPRESSION

Depression can often arise as a result of relationship breakdown. It can affect anyone from any background or social position and with various levels of confidence. We all go through ups and downs in life but doctors class it as depression when we have a low mood that continues each day for at least two weeks and becomes severe enough to interfere with day-to-day activities. Some examples of symptoms are:

- Life always seeming black.

- Feelings of guilt, worthlessness, or uselessness.

- Loss of enjoyment and interest in life, even of the hobbies and activities that we normally enjoy.

- Poor motivation. Even simple tasks seem difficult.

- Poor concentration. It may be difficult to read, work, etc.

- Sleeping problems.

- Lacking energy; always being tired.

- Poor appetite and weight loss, or maybe the opposite: comfort eating and weight gain.

Don't put up with these feelings on your own. The most important thing is to see a doctor and be honest about the emotions that you are experiencing. Depression arises for a number of reasons and may be linked to a chemical imbalance in your brain, and this is why antidepressants can be very effective. Simple things that can also help are:

- Taking exercise – this is a proven method of lifting the mood.

- Trying to eat regularly and eating healthy food.

- Not drinking alcohol, as this can easily depress you further.

- Not making big decisions – try to delay these for when you feel better.

SUICIDAL THOUGHTS

It is not uncommon for people to have suicidal thoughts when they are experiencing possibly the biggest crisis in their life. This is recent divorcee Bill's experience; his full story is given in more detail in Chapter 8.

> *About three years ago I was in a hotel that I often stay in when I am working. For no specific reason, the emotional storm clouds suddenly gathered and I just felt truly awful. Nothing in particular had sparked it off – I hadn't had an unpleasant phone call; there was no particular reason – it just happened that on that particular day I felt totally ghastly. I seriously considered taking the stairs to the fire exit at the top of the hotel and throwing myself off.*

At the time it surprised me even to be entertaining the thought of suicide, but I honestly contemplated finishing it at that point. I simply saw no end to the misery, the heartache, and the profound loneliness that comes with these situations. This was all made worse by the fact that my children were miles away and I hated not seeing them. I simply didn't see an end to the pain.

It was the thought of my children being told that their dad had died in that way (and the stigma that they would carry) that stopped me. At that point I thought, "No, damn it, I'm not going to give anybody the satisfaction of thinking they have gained some sort of perverse victory." So I resolved that I had to get through this. I didn't know how I was going to do it, but somehow I would.

When the immense strain of what you are feeling and dealing with is too much for you, it is natural sometimes to start to consider suicide. This is common among many people going through divorce. It is not that you are crazy, weak, or bad; it is simply that the burdens you are carrying are too much to bear.

If you are in this situation, I would make the following suggestions:

- Accept that you are not unusual. Relationship breakdown often brings great pain with it, but, like Bill, people do get through to make a full recovery.

- Don't do anything on the spur of the moment. Make a promise not to do anything for twenty-four hours or even a week. Feelings and actions are different – you may be feeling like this now, but you don't have to act on it.

- Stop taking drugs and alcohol – these make your negative thoughts worse.

- Talk to someone about your feelings. Relationship breakdown makes you feel alone and some people don't know how to react to this. However, there are many people who can help, such as your doctor and charities such as the Samaritans.

ACCEPTANCE

Many people react to the events that are happening to them with intense denial or disbelief. It's a natural self-protection mechanism, and you often hear people say, "I can't believe that they have done this to me." Sadly, the more you say this, the harder it is to deal with the real concerns in your life and move on. It is crucial to accept that the events that have occurred in your life have actually happened. This may sound silly, but acknowledging that, for example, unfaithfulness has taken place, your spouse is an addict, or your partner has said they don't want to be with you any more is very, very important.

It is also important to note here the difference between acceptance of past and future events. We all have to accept past events. Your relationship and your lives have changed. Change is here. Following that understanding, people may or may not make a judgment about what will happen in the future. Wondering whether a divorce will or will not occur in the future is about expectation, hope, and belief.

If you find it difficult to accept what is happening, two things can help you reach the stage of acceptance:

Why did it happen?

Firstly, understanding more about why the events happened can help people to accept that they are real. Were you able to talk well together? Did you both communicate your feelings? Were there problems that you never sorted out? Was your sex life good? Did you do things together? Why did you get married in the first place? What changed?

This is *not* to make you feel more guilty. No one has a perfect relationship and we all make mistakes; however, asking these questions will enable you to see the negative parts of your relationship and recognize the cracks that existed in your marriage. It may also help you to spot any areas in which you could have been a better partner.

Beware, though: sometimes we will never understand why things have happened. Therefore it's dangerous to become overly self-critical in your review of your relationship, as it can become a one-way street of what you did wrong. This is the experience of Katie:

> *My marriage ended because my husband had an affair. Although I wanted to try to make things work, he didn't. I felt so confused; I just couldn't see where things had gone so wrong. We loved each other, had fun together, rarely argued, and talked about our feelings on a regular basis. I was definitely in the "smug married" category for a while. I thought I had a good strong marriage and I thought we were both happy.*
>
> *When it ended, I started a desperate search for answers. I thought if I could just figure out what went wrong, I would feel at peace with it and be able to move on. I was also anxious that if I didn't understand why it had failed, I wouldn't be able to protect myself from a similar experience in the future.*
>
> *I spent a long time analysing everything, questioning everything I had said and done. When I couldn't find anything there, I started to doubt who I was – was there something about me that was intrinsically unlovable?*
>
> *Although I think some introspection is helpful and healthy, I went way beyond that. I didn't find answers or peace; I just knocked my self-confidence and started to hate who I was. I tried several times to get answers from my ex but I'm not sure he had any. Those conversations with him were painful, awkward, and fruitless. I don't think he knew what went wrong either – in fact, the most bizarre reason he came up with was that he had never bought me flowers. I am still not sure what he really meant by that.*
>
> *For me, learning to accept that I might never truly understand why my marriage failed has been an important part of my recovery.*

We can't control everything in life and sometimes, as the saying goes, bad things happen to good people. I think it is good to acknowledge our own failings and strive to be better, but it is equally important to know when to stop searching for answers.

Look at it from your ex's perspective

Secondly, trying to see the relationship from your partner's perspective will also help you to accept what has happened. I love the expression of one person:

"Standing in their shoes, however smelly they are, has helped me to move on."

Understanding more about your partner's background, their way of living, their family, and their approach to life can be of real benefit in helping you understand what's happened. Of course you may not agree with what they did, but it will increase your ability to accept what has happened.

Personal exercise

Have you accepted the events of the past?

Holding on to hope

However hard things are, I can assure you that there is hope.

At this time your confidence will have been dealt a huge blow. If your relationship has broken down, it's easy for you to feel uninteresting or unattractive. If one person has rejected you, it's easy to assume that everyone else will do so. You feel humiliated, ashamed perhaps, or a failure. However, this is *categorically untrue*. The *relationship* has failed, for whatever reason. But *you* are not a failure. You have other successful relationships, other gifts, talents, and skills.

A lot of people talk about feeling ill at ease with themselves or uncomfortable in public, whether at the school gate, at work, or in their social life. This is all normal. They are adjusting to a new set of circumstances.

I still hate the thought of having had a "failed marriage", of being just another statistic. Making mistakes in life does not mean that we are a failure.

I prefer Winston Churchill's view when he said, "No one fails; we just have more experience."

The important thing is not the past but rather that we learn from our experience to make the future better. If we can adapt and move on, then we have the opportunity to become stronger and build better relationships.

Some of my close friends have told me they believe that our friendship is now better because of the things that I learned as a result of my relationship breakdown. I would certainly not have chosen that route, but that is what happened. These comments highlight a crucial point: even though we may be feeling at the lowest point in our life, we can grow stronger through relationship breakdown, and this concept is something we can hold onto with hope.

Surviving from day to day

Dealing with all our feelings and the changing life around us can be very difficult. Even if we are able to make good plans for the long term, it can be hard to survive on a day-to-day basis.

I remember vividly the really dark moments that would come upon me from time to time when I was going through my separation. I remember one instance when I was travelling home from work: I felt this huge reservoir of blackness come over me. It swamped me for about twenty minutes. As I was parking my motorbike, a complete stranger walked past and asked me about my bike. We talked about bikes for about five minutes and then I walked into the house. Strangely, I did not feel the blackness at all any more.

I thought about this and realized that there is a power in distraction, in not focusing on our problems all the time. There is also power in human contact and in having common interests – which touches on our need for meaningful relationships.

This is one of the reasons why it is good to talk to someone who understands our situation. Not everyone comprehends the grave issues involved in relationship breakdown and we can easily become isolated and feel that no one else has these problems. That is why coming on a course with other people in the same situation can be so uplifting and rewarding. We can take the focus off ourselves as we hear about other people's situations, we can have human contact, and we can be distracted.

There are many other things that we can do to survive from day to day. Here are my top ten tips for getting through each day:

1. **Take one day at a time.** Drop the past, stop planning the future, and notice the present. I love the expression "Today is the first day of the rest of my life". "Today" is the most important day of your life, so try to make the most of it!

2. **Start writing a journal.** The mere process of writing down your thoughts and feelings can in itself be helpful. Don't endlessly contemplate your worst emotions, simply recognize them, as well as the things you find difficult and helpful. In due course, you will be able to look back and see how far you have moved on.

3. Understand that you are grieving. You are grieving the loss of your relationship. That grief will not last for ever as you begin to get used to your changed circumstances.

4. Try to appreciate others around you. Express your feelings to them; show them you care and let those close to you know how much you love them.

5. Be kind to yourself. Focus on rebuilding your self-confidence and limit the things that you find frustrating or difficult. Take up activities that you enjoy doing.

6. Count the good things in your life at the end of each day. There may be other people with even worse problems than yours. In my many trips to hospitals, during which I've often seen people in desperate situations, I am always reminded of this fact. Some people have found it helpful to write down the good things in their journal so that they can remember them when things get hard.

7. Enjoy laughter. It's OK to laugh even though the general situation is bad. It is said that children laugh about 400 times a day and adults only fifteen times. Laughing reduces muscular tension, improves breathing, regulates the heartbeat, and makes a great contribution to mental health. So watch some good comedy programmes and films (although obviously avoid those about adultery or relationship breakdown!).

8. Do some exercise. This doesn't have to be to get fit; it is just to get rid of the tension and stress that builds up in your body. Do whatever you can – a fifteen-minute quick walk is enough, and you will feel much better afterwards.

9. **Try to find time to help others.** You may feel that you have nothing to give at the moment, but maybe you could manage to smile at someone, listen to someone else's story, or call a person who is also finding life difficult. This is not meant to add more burdens to your life; it is a simple reflection that helping others, even in a small way, will help you.

10. **Seek help for the bigger problems that you pinpoint.** Don't be afraid of getting professional help when you are going through one of the hardest times that you will ever experience in your life.

Personal exercise

What would help you to get through the day? What could you instigate today?

Karina

Three and a half years ago, my husband and I separated and I did Restored Lives about six months later. I remember the first session: it was awful. The leader put up a big list of feelings and emotions. I felt all those things, every one of them, and I just sat and cried for the whole evening. I just couldn't believe the pain I was in. Every time someone spoke I began to cry again. I was very depressed, sad, broken, and thought I needed counselling as I felt stuck in a rut, endlessly trying to figure everything out in my head. That's how I normally dealt with things, but this time I couldn't manage it, so I went on the course and it helped.

What were the biggest challenges you were facing at the time?

I felt hugely betrayed and cheated, and I felt a lot of anger and a real loss of control. I have this belief that I can make things work and I don't give up on things. I had been trying for a long time in my marriage but unfortunately it hadn't worked and I couldn't accept it.

I felt angry about the fact that I had no control over what my husband felt and what he wanted to do. I also felt really alone, because I didn't grow up here, I grew up abroad where all my family live. I came here to go to university, married, and stayed here. I felt abandoned and that was a very big thing for me – coming to terms with being here on my own and being a single mum. That was a term that I really despised. I hated everything that went with what that meant or what I thought it meant: a sense of failure and shame.

All this happened at the beginning of the summer holidays and I remember taking the children to school in September. The first time I walked through the gates my heart was thumping; I felt as if there was a neon sign above me, flashing out: "Her husband has left her!" It was awful. My son was seven and my daughter only four, so both were suffering from the lack of attention. I sensed their pain too and felt like a real failure, and as if I was the only person going through this. The whole thing was bad.

What happened next?

I went back to work for a while, which really helped. Sadly, communication with my ex completely broke down. He began to make threats about money, so I went back to work for eight months. I was an accountant and I got a job for three days a week, which kept me from dwelling on myself or my problems for that space of time. Then coming on Restored Lives really helped too, as I realized I wasn't on my own. At the time there were forty or fifty people on the course, and I remember thinking, "Wow, there are other people going through this!" Nobody in my immediate circle was experiencing anything like it, and it really helped to feel that I wasn't alone and to know that all my feelings were normal.

I had all these horrible thoughts, and then made angry phone calls or crying phone calls. I was just a mess; I was so up and down. Coming on the course week after week was a wonderful way not to feel alone, to feel my emotions were valid, that they deserved to be expressed, and that I could heal them.

What were the keys steps to recovery?

A really important moment for me came when I was lying in bed and my brain just wouldn't stop working. I prayed that I would stop trying to fix everything. In my mind, yet as clearly as if I were really doing it, I picked up a box and put everything in it, then set it aside. It's my problem but I can't fix it, so I'm just going to leave it. That gave me real peace.

Then it became important for me to focus on wanting to repair our relationship enough for the children not to suffer in the long term. I remember saying to my husband, "I hope we will both be able to attend our children's weddings. I don't want them worrying, 'Are they fighting?'; 'Are they sitting next to each other?'; 'Has she come?'; 'Is he here?'" I knew it was a long way off but it was something I had to think about and work towards. I felt that if I had that goal, then at least I'd be able to take the steps to make our relationship work again, which meant forgiving him and forgiving myself. It made a huge difference.

What I did for a while was stop communicating with him, as I was so angry. I put certain boundaries in place, so if he was raging on the phone or there was swearing or shouting, I would warn him and then put the phone down. I sort of built protection around myself. I was then able to forgive him which allowed me not to think about him. I was able to move on, think about myself, and get on with my life.

How do you feel now?

It's a journey, a process, and it takes a long time. There will be dips, and sometimes the feelings of despair you had at the beginning return. But it gets better and you end up, as the journey of recovery shows, in a place that's stronger than where you first started.

My husband and I get on very well now. Although we're not together, we actually went on holiday with the children and it was the best holiday we'd ever had as a couple – that in itself is a miracle. We've rebuilt our relationship to a level at which we're good friends, and I think coming on the course was a key part of that. I had to go through that process of coming to terms with the break-up and being determined to move beyond it, but I'm stronger now and think I'm pretty close to the high point of the journey of recovery. It feels good.

TOOLBOX TO TAKE AWAY
Understanding the emotional impact

You can't change your ex but you can change yourself, and that will affect your future

Recognize your emotions – don't ignore them so that they become landmines ready to explode later on

Pinpoint the underlying problem – it's the first step in getting rid of it

Acceptance is important – have you accepted what's happened?

Have a day-to-day action plan – use the top ten tips suggested earlier in the chapter

PART TWO

BUILDING SELF-CONFIDENCE THROUGH COMMUNICATION

Chapter 3

Talking and listening

"I thought I was a pretty good communicator because I could talk a lot and I could give good advice to everyone…It took me a while to understand just how faulty my communication skills were."

Guy

"If I were to summarize in one sentence the single most important principle I've learned in the field of interpersonal skills, it would be this: seek first to understand, then to be understood."

Stephen Covey, *The 7 Habits of Highly Effective People*
(Franklin Covey, 2004)

Communication is the lifeblood of all relationships. If communication ceases, relationships get stuck. In view of all the emotions surging through you during separation and divorce, it is likely that communication will be difficult between you and your ex. But it doesn't always have to be like that, as there are a number of tools that can help you communicate.

These tools will give you more confidence and success in communicating with your ex. Importantly, they also help you prioritize the issues, and therefore give you more awareness and control of your life.

For some, it may be impossible to think positively about communication or conflict resolution with your ex because of your history. If your relationship has involved physical or verbal abuse, substantial deceit, addiction, or other mental health problems, this whole area can be very difficult. However, the principles given here apply equally to any relationship, so I would advise you not to miss this section out even if you will never talk with your ex again. In fact, improved communication is empowering and builds self-confidence in every area of life.

Blocks to good communication

It's not always easy to communicate well, particularly when dealing with our ex. Our feelings and the issues surrounding us will create a barrier to good communication. There are many blocks such as: anger, lies, emotional hurt, different opinions, stress of legal proceedings, financial worries, loss of trust, aggression, addictions, depression, fear, hidden agendas – the list goes on and on. Some of these come from our own feelings; some from our underlying fears; and others come from our ex's feelings and fears.

Let's look at a scene that demonstrates just how easily communication can go wrong.

The background to this scene is that it's Saturday morning and Kathy has had a difficult week. She is having a lie-in to fight off a headache. The doorbell rings. It's her ex, Robert:

Robert: *Can I come in? I need a quick word.*

Kathy: *Uh? Oh it's you... er, yeah, come in. Sorry it's a mess; I had Sarah round last night.*

Robert: *I've been checking our bank statement and I see that you've been using the joint account for your personal bills. You know we agreed that it would only be used for household bills.*

Kathy: *I've been really short this month so I had to use it. My car was about to run out of petrol. . . for goodness' sake, I've only done it once!*

Robert: *I don't care about the car. The fact is, we had a deal and you broke it. I'm going to tell the bank to freeze the account.*

Kathy: *You can't do that – how will I buy food? How will the mortgage get paid? Are you trying to get me out of the house? First I lose you and then I lose my home? I can't believe you'd do that to me! I'm already a wreck and the doctor says I need antidepressants. I love this house – you can't throw me out!*

Robert: *You should have thought about that before. You're just so chaotic – you've got to sort yourself out. Look at this kitchen – it's a mess. I'm not having you dip in and out of the joint account because you can't organize your money better. You can't be trusted with it.*

Kathy: *[Outraged] I can't be trusted? You have told me more lies in the last three months than I would have believed possible! How dare you tell me you can't trust me! You always think you can get away with whatever you want, don't you? You always think that you'll win. Well this time you're not going to win!*

That's a horrible scene, but one that can very easily take place. It highlights a number of the blocks and pitfalls that we can get ourselves into – here are a few of them:

• Kathy's emotions get in the way, as she fears losing her home.

- Robert is rude and confrontational.

- It is the wrong time and the wrong place for Kathy, but she still allows him in.

- Kathy doesn't respond to Robert's concern about the joint account.

- Robert brings up other issues: "You're just so chaotic."

- Kathy retaliates with allegations of lies.

- Kathy's reference to winning and losing is unhelpful and will make it harder to reach an agreement.

- All this is finished off with some personal attacks. All very unhelpful!

Personal exercise

What have been the biggest blocks to good communication between the two of you? When does your communication go wrong?

How to communicate well

The starting point for rectifying these situations is to understand that we can, and should, take responsibility for the way *we* communicate. We cannot alter anyone else (particularly our ex), but we *can* take responsibility for the way *we* choose to talk and listen. Do we help or aggravate the situation? Do we understand what they are saying or pour more fuel onto the fire? Taking responsibility for the way that we speak and respond is a critical starting place.

There are four important areas that form the foundation for being able to communicate successfully. These four areas will empower you to communicate more productively with your ex in whatever situation you may face and will help you not to fear meeting or speaking with them. They will create a strong platform from which you can start to resolve some of the differences that arise between you. They are:

1. Being aware of historical patterns of communication

2. Learning to express yourself: facts and feelings

3. Setting healthy boundaries

4. Seeking to be a good listener

1. Historical patterns of communication

We bring into any relationship ways of communicating that we learned from our family and our upbringing. Then, within their relationship, a couple will develop a way of behaving and communicating that becomes more "set". This set pattern is your historical pattern of communication. Some of these patterns of communication are healthy but some are unhealthy and will quickly increase the level of conflict and lead to unhelpful behaviour within the relationship.

Many of you will find that the first step in learning a new way of communicating is to press the pause button and give yourself some "time out". Once either one or both of you have started a separation or a divorce procedure, stop all communication with your partner for a certain time, let's say three weeks.

Why is this helpful? It enables you to stop and reflect on which patterns of communication are not working and are unhealthy for you. The unhealthier your past communications have been, the more important this stage of not communicating with your partner will be for you.

Some people may not need to do this because they can

still communicate well. However, if you have a high level of dependence on your ex or find yourself really keen to speak to them for no real reason, then this phase of not communicating will help you in the long run. Your relationship and communication have had a serious accident and need to start afresh. It's like rebooting the computer when it's crashed; it means you won't be able to use it for a short time.

Ceasing all communication forces you to stop and understand what has gone wrong. What is not working for me; what is not working for us as a couple? How can we communicate better? What are the unhealthy parts of our relationship and our communication? What do I need? What are the most important things in our lives? How can we best communicate to take care of the kids?

Maintaining communication with your partner throughout this period is often too difficult and distracting. You need to give yourself space and time to focus on these issues by yourself, together with supportive friends. The first days of doing this may be incredibly hard, but it will pay dividends in the long run. Just remember to tell your ex at the beginning that this is not a hostile step but will benefit both of you. This is your choice and it will strengthen you so that you can survive whatever decisions you both make in the future.

For people with children, those who work together, or those who still live in the same house – this means reducing communication to the absolute minimum. Keep everything else very businesslike: for example, speak about the children's travel arrangements and nothing else. Don't stop the ongoing contact arrangements with the children; just limit communication with your ex to the practical essentials.

For people who are keen to get back together and continue their marriage, it is vital to understand that any reconciled marriage must develop new patterns of communication, different to those before. Otherwise, it's doomed to failure. You also need to stop, reflect on what has not been working, and create new ways of talking together. To do that you need space and time away from the intensity of meeting and all the confusing messages that can be conveyed at this time. Do not fear pulling away for a short period. If a reconciled marriage is a possibility, then this process will be healthy for you and your partner, but make sure that you explain in a positive way that it is part of trying to solve your problems, rather than simply saying that you need to get away.

For some people, this period of non-communication will continue for a long time, particularly if they are in a very abusive relationship. For most people the goal is to reflect on unhealthy patterns of communication and then to re-engage in a different, more productive method of relating to one another, which will enable them to move forward more successfully.

Personal exercise

What unhealthy historical patterns of communication have you developed? Pause now to think about the types of communication that you want to stop and write them down here.

2. Learning to express yourself: facts and feelings

We express ourselves regularly each day and take the way we talk completely for granted. In the crisis of a relationship breakdown, it's helpful to take a moment to reflect on and understand how we express ourselves.

When we talk, we transmit both facts and feelings. The facts are the regular pieces of information about life, such as news, timings, schedules, plans, meetings, and events that we discuss every day. But these facts are shaped by our thoughts and feelings, which we express either explicitly or implicitly in the way we present the things we are communicating.

When you have a good relationship, there is an easy mix of facts and feelings. When a couple have separated or are in conflict and the relationship goes bad, it's essential to distinguish between the facts that need to be communicated to your ex and your feelings, which do not.

This table highlights the best way to communicate, depending on how well your relationship is working:

	Good relationship	Working relationship	Bad relationship
What we say	Easy mix of facts and feelings	Mostly facts	Just facts
Feelings expressed	Day-to-day and deeper feelings; hopes and dreams	Some "low-level" feelings	None

Your ex is someone with whom you have previously had a good relationship and been intimate. You probably told them everything, including your hopes and dreams. You now need to change the way you communicate with that person. It is no longer appropriate to share everything; instead, you have a new, more distant, relationship and must filter how and what you communicate.

In the scene we looked at earlier, Kathy was upset, and ended up telling Robert she was a wreck and that the doctor had advised her to start taking antidepressants. This was unnecessary information in the context of a discussion about the joint bank account.

The important step here is to recognize that the nature of the relationship has changed, and you need to adjust your communication to be more factual. You need to distinguish between what your feelings are (things that *you* need to deal with) and what the issues or facts are that need to be communicated to your ex.

DEALING WITH FEELINGS

But what do you do with all those feelings swirling around inside you?

You need a regular outlet for them. For most people, the best way is to have a "trusted friend" that you can talk to. This person may be someone close to you or it may be someone you don't know as well, such as a counsellor, mentor, coach, or vicar. They will listen, support, and, at times, challenge you. They are vital in your recovery process. If you don't have one at the moment, then I would encourage you to find someone, and in the meantime start writing a journal in which you can begin to express these thoughts and feelings – they need to come out somehow!

Men sometimes have a reputation for being less willing to express feelings, but this is not a gender-specific issue – both men and women can find it difficult. The important point to remember is that in a complex emotional situation your mind literally cannot work it all out by itself, and having someone else to talk to will accelerate your recovery as well as enabling you to communicate more easily with your ex.

It is always difficult to change the way you have previously communicated with someone and it needs practice. However, by keeping feelings out of the conversation, you will be making communication with your ex less highly charged, less driven by your emotional state, and more focused on the real practical matters.

Personal exercise

What are the facts or concerns that need to be communicated to your ex at the moment? What are the feelings that you need to deal with elsewhere?

3. Setting healthy boundaries

In the same way that the walls of the house provide us with physical refuge, the emotional boundaries we place around our relationships provide us with an emotional refuge. If our house has been burgled, we may need to put in some new security measures in order to protect ourselves and increase our feeling of safety. We can do the same for the emotions arising out of our relationships.

When a relationship has broken down, the person with whom we have shared the greatest intimacy must now become someone whose access to us – both physical and emotional – needs to be restricted and changed. Hopefully we won't literally have to change the locks on our home, but we *will* need to change our emotional locks in order to make ourselves less accessible. Having a definite line in the sand regarding what's appropriate and what's not, is called "setting a boundary".

The concern for most people in this type of situation is not physical safety but emotional safety. In the scene, Kathy allowed Robert to come into the house, even though she was not expecting him and was not feeling well. He was allowed to gain access to her personal space and he abused this privilege. After commenting on the mess in the kitchen, Robert proceeded to make a personal insult about Kathy being chaotic, resulting in her feeling wretched. She needed to have some boundaries in place to protect her from this verbal abuse and the emotional impact that results.

The extent to which boundaries are necessary will depend entirely on how well the relationship is going. Boundaries can be adjusted. When things are very difficult and we feel vulnerable, the boundaries may be quite restrictive (such as not communicating with someone, for example). If we get on well with someone, the boundaries can be more relaxed – perhaps they can come into the house, but not to eat or stay for a long time. The boundaries may need to be quite strict during the early months of a separation, then, all being well, becoming more relaxed as the relationship gets easier.

Another example of a boundary is when a couple have separated and there are tense moments when the children are being picked up and dropped off. In this instance, it may be appropriate for one of the parents to say they will not discuss any problems when handing over the children. If this is not respected, the boundary will have to be reinforced, possibly by stopping the other parent from coming up to the house. For example you would say: "If you are not willing to respect my request that we don't discuss issues when dropping off the kids, then in future wait in the car and I will bring the children out to you." However unreasonable this may seem to the other person, it may be necessary for a while, in order to avoid stress and a possible scene in front of the children.

Examples of other potentially necessary boundaries include:

- "You may no longer ring me at the office unless there is an emergency."

- While on the phone: "I can't talk to you if you shout and scream at me. I will ring you back in thirty minutes when you have calmed down."

One woman spoke of what happened shortly after her husband left her, when a very close family friend died. She said:

I was very upset. My separated husband came round and he was also very upset. He wanted to hug me but I would not let him – it would have been too difficult to cope with that moment of intimacy, only for him to go off again afterwards. A hug would have crossed a boundary that I had to keep in place for my own emotional safety.

There are two things to be learned from these examples:

Firstly, you may have to tell those affected that you are putting a boundary in place and you have to be clear what that boundary is.

Secondly, the other person may not welcome the restriction, making it difficult for you to be firm. Remember that just because a boundary is unpopular, it does not mean it is wrong. If you are certain that the boundary is reasonable and appropriate for your situation, then it should be put in place. It is essential to remember not to remove the boundary if it is challenged; instead, make sure you have the necessary support and encouragement from others to keep it intact.

Be sure to look at the implications of your boundary from the receiving end as well. Discuss it with a friend or counsellor in order to work out whether it is reasonable or whether there may be a better way. If a boundary that is imposed on you doesn't seem fair, you could try to discuss it with your ex and invite them to consider an alternative one that is easier to respect.

Personal exercise

Are there any boundaries that you would like to put in place?
How has it been to have a boundary line imposed on you?

4. Good listening

The art of being a good listener is not particularly well recognized or valued in today's world. Stephen Covey, an international expert and author on the subject of communication, said this:

> *If I were to summarize in one sentence the single most important principle I've learned in the field of interpersonal skills, it would be this: seek first to understand, then to be understood.*
> Stephen Covey, *The 7 Habits of Highly Effective People*
> (Franklin Covey, 2004)

Many of the problems that arise in communication can be resolved by learning to listen. Many people think they are good communicators, but they often just mean that they express themselves well. To be a good communicator, you also need to be a good listener.

It may sound strange even to say, "How do we learn to listen?" – it is a skill that requires focus and practice.

REFLECTIVE LISTENING

We can practise listening by going through an exercise called "reflective listening". It's a very useful method of listening that enables the listener to understand the core issues quickly and empowers the speaker to clarify the issues in their mind. These are the key things to do:

1. **Pay attention.** Do not do anything else at the same time, and maintain eye contact even if you feel uncomfortable.

2. **Listen without interrupting.** We need to forget about our own agenda and opinions. This means not interrupting, and allowing the other person to say what

they want to. This can be very difficult, as we all build up bad listening habits. Try not to:

* interrupt;
* give advice or try to solve the problem ("What you ought to do is this…");
* go off at a tangent ("That reminds me of that TV programme…");
* refer it back to yourself ("Oh, I remember when that happened to me…");
* intellectualize ("Psychologists have proved that's not true!").

3. Reflect back what is being expressed, particularly their thoughts and feelings. Using the <u>same words</u> the speaker has used enables the speaker to know that the listener really understands how they feel. It also gives the speaker the chance to say, "No, **this** is what I really meant."

4. After listening and reflecting back, ask two things:

i) "What is the most important thing in what you have said?";

ii) "Is there anything you would like to do about it?"

This provides the person with a framework for coming up with his or her own solution.

Reality check: *I initially struggled with using this tool, as it seemed artificial and quite unlike a normal conversation. I also have a very bad short-term memory and would forget the exact words people had used, which made me feel slightly embarrassed. On top of that,*

I love helping people if I have experience of a similar situation (i.e. I have a talent for interrupting and offering advice).

But what constantly surprises me is the reaction of people who have tried out this skill. We try out this skill on the course and then ask people what it felt like to be listened to in this manner. These are some of the responses:

I felt valued; it clarified things in my mind; I felt that I was interesting; I felt understood; I felt empowered to act; I felt respected; I felt important; it was healing; I came to a conclusion on an issue; it felt refreshing; I felt affirmed; I felt worth something.

It is amazing to get such responses merely from having a person listen to you and repeat what you have said. Responses such as, "I felt important" and "It was healing" show the real power of just being listened to.

This tool also works in other environments where something is important, complicated, or tense. It's not to be used all the time (otherwise life would grind to a halt), but I have tried it in crisis situations at work, with kids, or with my friends, and it really helps – give it a try!

The reason that this tool is so powerful is that at the heart of listening lies valuing the other person enough to put down our own agenda and let them become the centre of our world for a moment. The attitude of the listener must be that the other person's view is the important one; their experience is the one that matters; their perspective is a valid one; and their solution is more important than our advice. When this happens there is healing in being listened to because people feel important and therefore valued. It moves from being a listening exercise to a matter of restoring people's self-esteem and belief in themselves. Luckily we can all do it, and then we can start to train people to return the favour to us.

Personal exercise

Try reflective listening with someone next time a discussion arises on something complicated or significant. If you need to be listened to yourself, find someone you know who listens well, or say to a friend, "Can you just listen today and not try to sort me out?"

Remember to ask the questions: "What is the most important thing for you?" and "Is there anything you would like to do about it?"

Summary

Learning to communicate well is empowering: it can improve many aspects of our lives and is one of the single most important elements in building self-confidence.

When we are going through a relationship breakdown the flood of feelings and emotions may overwhelm us and will have a negative impact on our ability to think straight. At this stage, being able to focus on the core elements of communication – being able to express yourself and being able to listen – will empower you in a remarkable way. As it increases your sense of being valued, it grows the seeds of hope and is therefore a vital part of the journey of lifting you out of the valley of despair.

These tools then become key skills to help you resolve conflict, either in your everyday life or in the bigger ongoing battles of divorce, such as finances and arrangements for the children.

Guy

After I met Tania we spent two years getting to know each other before we got married. When we got together there was lots of love. We had some great times and shared a lot of wonderful adventures, including setting up a new business, which seemed to be going well.

I thought I was a pretty good communicator because I could talk a lot and I could give good advice to everyone. I'm sad to say that I had all the things on the list of inappropriate methods of communication, but the trouble was I didn't know that I was communicating in a bad way. I was using patterns that I'd learned and had seen played out in my family, which had weak emotional boundaries between its members.

From the start we had a complicated relationship with her mum and dad. In addition, Tania had a very difficult relationship with my mum because my mum was quite critical and negative – I really felt for Tania on that score.

It was only a couple of months into the marriage when Tania's parents, who had had quite a lot of financial problems, turned to me and said, in effect, "Right, you're now fully responsible for supporting us. We've lost our money and we want you to pay for everything." I was really shocked, as we'd only been married a short time and we had just set up a new business, which wasn't earning any money yet. It was a very conflictual time for me as my heart went out to them because of the situation they'd got themselves into, but equally I thought that I had to protect my new marriage.

Then, when we'd been married for just over a year, the cracks started appearing and communication and boundaries all became huge problems for us.

I remember when I first turned to Tania and said it wasn't working. I should have timed it better. We'd been on holiday to Italy and were making our way back by train – it was a lousy idea to decide to talk during this tiring fourteen-hour journey. I was looking out of the window and I turned round to her and said, "This really isn't working." What I'd meant to say was that we had a lot of things we needed to sort out. But it came out as "This isn't working" as if it were already finished, and that was the end of things for her.

We tried to reconcile at various times, including by going on The Marriage Course, but it didn't work and the whole process got very complicated. When the separation finally happened it was phenomenally painful but, in another way, it came as a relief.

It took me a while to understand just how faulty my communication skills were, and even today there are still many areas where I'm a work in progress. I began to develop the ability to see things from other people's perspectives. There were lots of other problems – I used to interrupt and give advice; I used to approach everything from the perspective of my own experience – and all these started to change.

I began to learn to listen and I began to understand what boundaries were and how to establish them successfully. I had to establish huge boundaries with my mum over the divorce and at first it was a very painful thing to do. It was hard for me to institute it, as I had complex concerns about whether I was doing the right thing.

But my efforts were rewarded handsomely in the sense that the consequences were really helpful and our relationship is far better now than at any time since my teenage years. I have a really great relationship with my mum now because I had to model good communication, listening skills, and boundaries to her and then, as I changed, she too changed for the better. I now enjoy a lot of good communication in my relationships and it's been a journey of hope.

TOOLBOX TO TAKE AWAY
Talking and listening

Recognize your own blocks to good communication

Take responsibility for the way you speak and respond

Pause – check for historical unhealthy patterns of communication and behaviour

Your relationship has changed, so the way you express yourself must change too: use facts not feelings

Don't ignore feelings: have an outlet for them, such as talking to a trusted friend

Use emotional boundaries to protect your heart and mind

Practise reflective listening: it helps both you and your ex-partner

Chapter 4

Conflict resolution

"Communication in the last ten years was severely lacking, and conflict resolution non-existent. We would end up having a major battle and then go to sleep. She would wake up having forgotten all about it, which I found very frustrating…

"I have learned just how important it is not to let things fester…

"…to focus on what the key issue was, so there was no distracting blame game and anger. In fact, it's worked well, and in the last few months we've actually started discussing things verbally, which is quite something."

Benjamin

Even if both parties express themselves and listen perfectly there will still be differences of opinion, and these can lead to conflict. Sadly, most of us are a long way away from perfection and the reality is that most relationship breakdowns involve a substantial degree of communication breakdown with often zero conflict resolution.

The response to conflict can range from silence and resigned acceptance through to rage and lots of arguments. This represents the two ends of the spectrum when dealing with conflict: firstly, avoiding disagreements whenever possible (often because of fear); and, secondly, arguing but never resolving the problems. Both of these responses are dangerous and both are present in epidemic proportions throughout society today; it requires courage to overcome them when experiencing personal conflict.

Fortunately, if you have the will, there are a number of tools that can enable you to be less fearful of conflict and give you an excellent chance of resolving issues successfully. These tools become like a solid framework that you can hold on to in the midst of the storms of argument.

What is conflict resolution?

Conflict resolution is *not* about attack by one person and surrender by the other. You need to leave behind the idea of winning and losing, as this will lead only to more polarized positions and further conflict.

Conflict resolution entails understanding each other's concerns about something and **finding a solution that works for both of you**.

So what can you do? Here are five practical steps that will help you.

Step 1: Choose your attitude

This first step involves looking at your attitude. You need to **choose** to handle conflict in a productive way. It is all about attitude – you can choose to fight or you can be a peacemaker. Decide that you are not going to retaliate or fuel the conflict at all.

When something triggers a reaction within you there is often a split second during which you can choose the way that you respond. It's at this moment you need to shout "Time out!", hit the pause button, and channel your feelings in a different direction. This will help you to choose how you react.

> *I have a friend who is living with serious stress because all the financial and practical consequences of her marriage breakdown have yet to be resolved. Various events have taken place that have upset and annoyed her hugely. Her instinctive reaction is anger with a plan for revenge: "Right, if that's how you want it, then I'll. . ." Each time this happens, she lets off steam to me or a close member of her family and then seeks to take a more rational and less confrontational approach with her husband. She holds on to the premise that it is better for her and her children to handle conflict in a productive way and it remains her choice to do so.*

Step 2: What's the issue?

One of the worst side effects of relationship breakdown is that people can feel robbed of their ability to think calmly and make good decisions because there are so many things going on at once. Uncertainty about the future can be overwhelming, and a sense of mental chaos can take hold.

If you have an argument it is common for one issue to lead to another, and then to another (probably unrelated) matter. These are then finally finished off with some critical comments about the person's character, just like Robert and Kathy in Chapter 3. In this situation, each person will bring three or four different concerns together, trying to make a bigger and bigger mountain, as if aiming to overcome the opposition through sheer quantity. This is when it is especially easy to give up, with a wall of problems between the two of you which all appear unresolvable.

We can tackle only one issue at a time. We therefore have to work out which is the most important one to resolve now and then leave the others for another day. I love this quote from Winston Churchill: "It is a mistake to look too far ahead. Only one link in the chain of destiny can be handled at a time."

Reflective listening with a friend is really helpful in finding which issue to resolve first. Talk to your friend about the conflict that you are in and answer the question, "What is the most important thing in what you have said?" Then, having identified the key issue, try to clarify why you and your ex are in disagreement over it.

Once you are speaking with your ex, reflective listening is again an extremely helpful way of finding out what they think the most important thing is. You don't have to guess what the real issue is; just ask them. You don't necessarily have to agree with what they say, but you will understand the situation better. Interestingly, this tactic also gives you more time to think about how you are going to respond.

In the scene with Kathy and Robert in the previous chapter, Kathy never found out what the most important matter was from Robert's perspective, and the discussion quickly spiralled out of control into allegations of chaotic living, lack of trust, and lying.

Step 3: Find the best time and place to communicate

The third step is to find the best time and place to communicate. This is critical, as there are times and places at which positive conflict resolution is impossible. In the scene mentioned above, it was both a bad time and a bad place for Kathy.

I know one couple who were sitting next to each other in a school hall waiting for their son's school play to start. One of them raised a query about something controversial and asked the other to agree – it was disastrous. It was neither the right time nor the right place.

So you need to agree on a time that works for both of you. There may be a week when you or your ex feel too vulnerable and can't manage it. Don't allow yourself to be pushed – you can wait for a time that suits you both (provided that it is not put off endlessly).

Then think of where the discussion should take place. It could be face to face, at home, or in a neutral venue such as a coffee shop. Many people find that meetings at home are too reminiscent of how things were when they were a couple – a neutral venue reduces the possibility of unhelpful emotions being stirred up and can make it easier to focus on the matter in question.

Alternatively, your discussion could take place over the telephone, or these days many people communicate by email. I know one couple who manage all their arrangements by text message, as they find they have less confrontation that way. Think creatively about what would work best for the two of you and suggest it to your ex in a positive way.

Step 4: Confront the issue, not each other

The mountain of concerns brought by each person quickly moves from the issue in question to being an attack on one of their characters, leading inevitably to a volcanic explosion (either verbally or internally). The scene in Chapter 3 ended up with Kathy shouting, "You always think you can get away with whatever you want, don't you? You always think that you'll win. Well this time you're not going to win!"

Saying "You always…" or "You never…" is aggressive and personal, and fuels the fire. More importantly, these statements are *never* wholly true, so simply lead to more arguments.

As you discuss all the issues, try to avoid making personal accusations, even if you are attacked. Statements that begin with "You" are likely to confront the person rather than the problem. Therefore, statements using "I" or "My" are far better: "I want to make sure the timing for the kids' pick-up works", or "I switch off when you shout at me."

Most people have perfect recall of unkind comments made during arguments because they are painful and stick in the mind for a long time. Personal accusations simply double your trouble, as the underlying reason for an argument is missed and a far more dangerous issue is raised, about the person's character.

Instead, confront the issue and keep coming back to the nub of it. Don't make general comments but find a specific example of when the problem occurred and look at what actually took place. Analyse this specific matter and work out what was happening there, why you got upset, and what the emotional trigger was that set things off.

If you do not have a good relationship with your ex, restrict communication to the facts of the situation and relate them to the impact they have on you or the children: "If you are late picking Alice up from our house then I might miss my appointment, which will cost us money."

If your relationship is working a little better, you can express it using "I feel…" sentences: "When you are late picking Alice up, it makes me feel anxious and fearful."

I have found that sitting next to the other person and visualizing the problem as if it were in front of you both is hugely helpful. If two people are sitting opposite each other, any discussion of an issue that's between them quickly seems to turn into an attack on one or the other.

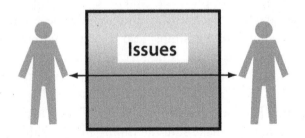

If, instead, the two people sit next to each other (or at right angles if they can't cope with that!), with the issue on a piece of paper in front of them, they can focus more easily on the matter at hand rather than feeling attacked by the other person.

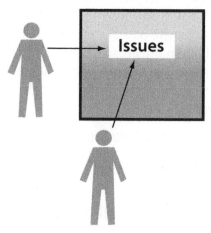

That's why discussing something while sitting at the corner of a table or walking is less aggressive and will make discussion less personal. It's a helpful tool for keeping you both focused on the issue rather than on the other person.

Step 5: Problem-solve to reach a solution that's good for both of you

Once you have identified the most important problem, think creatively about possible solutions to it. Consider these solutions with a friend and remember to look at the matter from your ex's perspective as well. Then you can discuss it with your ex in a healthier manner.

Don't worry if the first solution doesn't work and you have to try a number of different ideas over time. That's very normal when dealing with difficult issues.

Look for outside inspiration. Don't be frightened of trying something new, such as getting help from a third party – maybe a family member, a mutual friend, a church leader, or a professional mediator. Conflict breeds conflict and you can easily get stuck in a negative spiral. Seeking outside help and inspiration is one way of halting this downward trend. If you do bring in a supportive outsider, make it clear to your ex that your aim is to find a mutually acceptable solution, and you feel that you need some help in order to do this successfully.

Personal exercise

Which of these steps would help you in your conflict resolution? Who could help you find a solution?

Putting it all together

Can all this make a difference? Absolutely! Even in the toughest of circumstances, if you take responsibility for the way *you* communicate, you increase the likelihood of a better response from your ex and therefore increase the chances of resolving your conflict.

The combination of healthy communication and a structure for resolving conflict makes a massive difference (I have tried both ways!). Being able to listen and express yourself well sends a message of respect and value to the other person and is therefore the beginning of building a bridge between you. Then the ability to focus on the main issue, and brainstorming to find the best solution, enables you to complete the bridge and arrive at a good solution for both of you.

Let's see what would have happened if Kathy had read this chapter and implemented these ideas.

On the day that Kathy has used the joint account to pay for her personal expenses, she has a nagging awareness in her mind that she has done something wrong. She doesn't dismiss this feeling; instead, she sends Robert an email explaining her actions. She also suggests that they meet in a coffee shop after work to talk about money. Before she meets Robert, Kathy discusses with a trusted friend what she would like to say to him. Her friend imagines how Robert might respond and they rehearse how this difficult meeting might go. Kathy approaches the meeting feeling well prepared but a little nervous.

Kathy: *Thank you for coming, Robert. I wanted to talk to you about money. As you know, I used the joint account to pay for something personal. I did it because a payment hadn't cleared into my own bank account, but I know that it was outside what we agreed.*

Robert: *I can't believe you did that. We had an agreement – how can I trust you if every time you need a bit of spare cash you dip into the joint account? I'm going to tell the bank to freeze it.*

Kathy: *I understand that you can't believe what I did and I'm sorry for doing it. [pause] OK, you're thinking of freezing the account.*

Robert: *Yes – we just can't have this happening again!*

Kathy: *Is that the most important thing here for you?*

Robert: *Well, the problem was that we nearly went past the overdraft limit that the bank agreed, which will not help me get the mortgage for that flat I'm trying to buy. How can I trust you to use the money I put in the joint account for the right things? The reality is, Kathy, that you have never been organized and you always live in chaos.*

Kathy: *[pause] I don't think it will help either of us if we get personal. I am not going to sit here while you are rude to me and I am not about to be rude to you. We have a financial matter to resolve – let's keep it at that. Now, about the joint account: you're worried that we will spend more than we have agreed and will exceed the overdraft limit – is that right?*

Robert: *Yes – well look what happened this week!*

Kathy: *Would it help if I tell you when I start running out of money and give you advance warning of when I need to use the joint account funds? I am happy to promise that I will only use the joint account for personal expenses if we have spoken first and agreed it – so you know what's going on.*

Robert: *OK. That would be reassuring, for the time being. But I do want to get on and sort out our money, once and for all, so we don't have to go on having this sort of conversation.*

Kathy: *I agree. Let's ring that mediator who was recommended to us. Hopefully, we can arrange the first meeting with him soon. In the meantime, I promise to let you know if my account gets low and I need to use our joint account.*

So what did she do?

- Kathy met at a good time and place, and felt ready.

- A boundary was made clear: "I am not going to sit here while you are rude to me and I am not about to be rude to you".

- Kathy kept it purely factual and did not retaliate even when provoked twice with the word "trust".

- Kathy used reflective listening to make sure that Robert knew she understood his concern.

- She got more information out of him by using reflective listening and found out the underlying reason why he was angry – the bank might not give him a mortgage.

- She kept the discussion focused on the main point rather than reacting to Robert's unkind words.

The final step

The final step in conflict resolution is often overlooked. It's the process of letting go of any emotional damage that has arisen between two people when in conflict.

Even if you have achieved a good solution, if the process has been difficult and unkind words have been spoken, these will act like landmines in your communication and your relationship in the future.

We will look at the process of letting go in more detail in the next two chapters.

Benjamin

I was married for twenty-three years and a year ago we finally got divorced. We had a very tough last year and a half because we had to live under the same roof. Conflict resolution and communication was a skill set I could have done with; I certainly didn't have it at the time.

What was the most painful part of your experience?

I have a son who is twenty and two daughters, who are seventeen and twelve. The worst thing for me was suddenly going from being in a family unit to being in a flat and seeing them only once every couple of weeks. It was hard selling the family home, particularly as my younger daughter and I are very close. She was so young and then suddenly our whole relationship changed.

Having said that, one year on it's working well and the children are settled. Though I don't live with them, the time I spend with them is very special.

Was it difficult to communicate with your ex?

Definitely. Communication in the last ten years was severely lacking, and conflict resolution non-existent. We would end up having a major battle and then go to sleep. She would wake up having forgotten all about it, which I found very frustrating. But that was our pattern, particularly in the last year.

I have learned just how important it is not to let things fester, which was certainly what happened.

In the early days, during and after the divorce process, my communication with my ex was just by email and text. I think doing that helped us to focus on what the key issue was, so there was no distracting blame game and anger. In fact, it's worked well, and in the last few months we've actually started discussing things verbally, which is quite something.

I was also unsure of what was reasonable on my part as regards boundaries and I found it very helpful to discuss this with a third party. Then when I was in a discussion with my ex, I was more able to stand firm on some things and know when to give in on others. I certainly found that very useful at the time.

How did you live together for a year during the divorce process?

It was very tough; we'd actually take turns to be in the house at weekends. She met a new partner within a month, which I found quite difficult, but as a result I was happy to do more of the weekends with the children, which seemed to work out. We were glad when the house sale finally went through. It was very traumatic packing up, but a relief that we could all start again.

What helped you at the hardest times?

When I first came on the course I really was in the depths of despair. What helped me first was coming on the course. Second, a friend invited me to go to a therapist he had been to. It really helped, having a chance each week to open up and discuss issues that I didn't feel I could talk about with my friends.

The other big thing was that we could have got very embattled in the divorce proceedings, but in fact we went to mediation and after attending seven sessions over a year we weren't in conflict and we came to a happy conclusion. We had both been to a lawyer beforehand and immediately took up positions that were way apart. We sat down with the mediator and realized that after twenty-three years we had grown apart, and therefore what was taking place was for the best. We realized that the children came first and that it was OK to have a few differences along the way. The mediator got us to sit down and discuss the issues and we certainly came to a much happier, speedier conclusion than we would have done otherwise.

What stage are you at now?

I feel that I am a reasonable way along on the journey. I've hit many bumps, such as when the children went on holiday with the new partner for the first time, but I look at them as milestones on the road. The first one is very hard, but gradually it gets easier. I certainly feel that things are moving on and I am in a much better place now.

TOOLBOX TO TAKE AWAY
Conflict resolution

When you have a disagreement, hold on to this framework:

Step 1: *Choose your attitude*
 — *be a peacemaker even if your ex isn't*

Step 2: *What's the issue?*
 — *tackle only one issue at a time*

Step 3: *Find the best time and place to communicate*
 — *think about a neutral venue*

Step 4: *Confront the issue, not each other*
 — *don't use "You never…" or "You always…"*
 — *place the issue in front of you, not between you*

Step 5: *Problem-solve to reach a solution that's good for both of you*
 — *keep trying new solutions*
 — *look for outside inspiration*

Step 6: *Let go (read on…)*

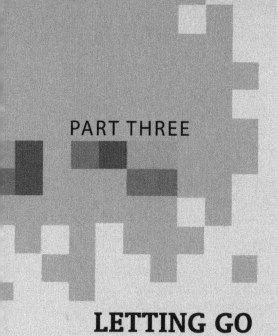

PART THREE

LETTING GO

Chapter 5

Freedom from the past

*"I felt that I had to forgive… I did, and it was a
real turning point in my life. I changed. It changed
the way I feel about myself, and what I felt about
Edward and what he'd done wrong. I had built up
a fairy-tale existence in my mind: nice job, lovely
partner, good lifestyle, etc., and the break-up of our
relationship caused it to tumble down around me.
I was standing in the ruins of my own castle and it
was like a prison. I had to forgive to break out of that
prison, break through the rubble, and get out into
the big wide world."*

Jodie

The communication and conflict resolution strategies we
have looked at are vital elements of creating a better working
relationship with our ex. They help us to understand ourselves
and others better. However, no matter how good these skills
are, they will not stop the pain and the hurt from what has
happened. The single most important ingredient in letting go
of this emotional damage is forgiveness.

Forgiveness stops us being tied to the past and gives us

hope for the future. Most importantly, forgiveness helps us to make better choices and opens the door to a new relationship, free from the effects of past hurt. It gives us new life and freedom to move on.

Despite all the good that it does, forgiveness is still one of the most misunderstood concepts that I know of and it can mean many different things to different people.

I love this story (most likely apocryphal) about Pánfilo de Narváez, the Spanish soldier and explorer, who died in 1528. As Narváez lay dying, his father confessor asked him whether he had forgiven all his enemies, explaining that the Bible says: "If you forgive men when they sin against you, then your heavenly Father will also forgive you." Narváez looked astonished and said, "Father, I have no enemies... I have shot them all."

Like Narváez's "shoot-them-first" attitude, many people's first reaction to the suggestion that they should forgive is "There is no way I will let them off the hook for what they've done!" or "It wouldn't be fair to forgive them", or maybe "I can't even forgive myself for my actions".

Many of us feel great apprehension about the topic of forgiveness. Sometimes the shock of separation is so great that we need time to absorb it and let the powerful emotions subside a little.

That was certainly the case for me. My relationship changed overnight without warning. It took me a while to work out what was going on, and much longer to find out some of the reasons why it was happening. Initially my pain was too much to bear, so letting go and forgiving were not things I could even consider. I've since found out that these feelings are very normal.

However, whatever your situation and whatever your preconceptions about forgiveness, I want to encourage everyone to have a fresh look at the subject over the next two chapters.

What does forgiveness mean?

We all carry ingrained notions of what forgiveness means. Some people feel that it is very unnatural. Others hold that you can't forgive someone unless that person accepts their wrongdoing, is punished, apologizes fully for it, and repairs the harm done.

Perhaps you have read about the former UK cabinet minister Norman Tebbit, whose wife was paralysed as a result of the Brighton bomb that was planned and planted by Irishman Patrick Magee in 1984. Tebbit has still not forgiven Magee because he does not believe he has done enough to earn forgiveness. This is Tebbit's choice, and it should be respected. He said this:

> I could forgive them if they showed any contrition, regret or remorse, but I can't forgive someone who justifies what Magee did. The world spins on so quickly that the pressure on these victims to forgive and forget verges on the obscene.

> *Daily Mail* online, 24 July 2009

In the same incident, there were also ordinary members of the public who were injured or killed. Jo Berry lost her father. But she has forgiven Magee. She even has empathy and compassion towards him.

These are two very different responses to the same person, for the same act. I want to talk about how you can apply Jo Berry's approach to forgiveness in your own life, and why it is the best way for you to let go of the pain and the hurt that you have experienced.

Personal exercise

What's your view of what forgiveness means and achieves?

Is forgiveness just for religious people?

Some people believe that forgiveness is purely part of a religious understanding of life. However, having worked with people both with and without faith, I am convinced that the freedom that forgiveness brings is open to everyone, irrespective of their religious beliefs. Perhaps this is because it reflects a deeper universal truth within each of us and within our relationships.

There are examples of forgiveness from a religious perspective, such as the attitude of Jesus, who calls us to forgive all those who have hurt us. But there are also examples from a non-religious point of view and many people come on the course with no religious beliefs but have experienced the same freedom.

Numerous other authors from different backgrounds have written about it:

- Louise L. Hay's book *You Can Heal Your Life* (Hay House, 2004) has sold over 35 million copies, and in it she says: "To release the past, we must be willing to forgive."

- Francine Kaye in *The Divorce Doctor* (Hay House UK, 2009), says this of forgiveness: "It will change your attitude to your life and will manifest itself through all the actions you take, and will allow you to heal your heart and love again."

- Steve Maraboli, author, coach, and radio-show host, says this in *Life, The Truth, and Being Free* (Better Today Publishing, 2009): "The truth is, unless you let go, unless you forgive yourself, unless you forgive the situation, unless you realize that that situation is over, you cannot move forward."

Many of the personal stories highlight the impact of forgiveness and some of them make reference to God; however, if you have no belief in God, take it simply as another example of the effectiveness of forgiveness from a different perspective.

As we look more deeply into the subject of forgiveness, I will leave aside any specific religious arguments.

Why should we think about forgiving?

There are two compelling reasons why we should forgive others.

1. Revenge does not work

The first reason for forgiving is that revenge does not work. We all have an instinctive desire for justice, and when we have been wronged we feel it is only right that the perpetrator should suffer in some way. Sometimes there is a part of us that wishes to bring about justice by inflicting the punishment ourselves.

I remember reading the story of Lady Sarah Graham-Moon, who was in the process of separating from her husband. In retaliation for his affair, she cut the sleeves off all his Savile Row suits, threw paint all over his BMW car, and deposited his vintage wine collection on neighbours' doorsteps. She said,

> *In retrospect I do think that it was a bit over the top. I did it to relieve my own intense hurt and frustration.*
>
> *The Times* newspaper, 29 May 1992

We can all relate to that feeling. While we may understand the motive for actions such as these, the problem is, if we set out on this route, we can easily get out of control. Regularly we hear of much sadder stories where a relationship has broken down and one partner's desire for revenge has resulted in a desperate act.

I read the story of Julia Wright, a woman who stabbed her husband's mistress to death. The prosecution said:

> *There were two pillars that supported Mrs Wright's life: the love of her husband whom she believed could do no wrong, and the love of her four children. She was driven to kill by the fear that, having taken over her husband, his mistress was about to take over her children as well.*
>
> The Times *newspaper, 3 December 1994*

Vengeful acts can never compensate for the harm that's been caused by a relationship breakdown and they don't release that intense frustration that you feel. What act can relieve the hurt caused by the person who has, for instance, betrayed you by sleeping with someone else, the spouse who has ruined the last ten years of your life by being an addict, or the partner who has taken your children away?

Often, the person who feels wronged simply holds on to their pain. With no outlet, it continues to grow inside them and causes more and more problems.

The first reason why we should try to forgive is that revenge, and all the bad thoughts and feelings that are associated with it, simply does not work.

2. We lose out

The second reason is that, if we do not forgive, we ourselves lose out. Lack of forgiveness will affect every area of our life. It's like perpetually carrying a large piece of baggage on our shoulders.

Not forgiving means:

- We are affected physically – we don't stand properly.

- We are affected emotionally – we don't smile as much.

- We are worn out by the burden – we become irritable.

- We can become ill – physical or mental illness can be a consequence.

- Our choices about what we do are affected – "I can't take anything else on as I'm already weighed down with this baggage."

- Our choices about whom we talk to are also affected – "I'm not going to talk to that person because they look like the one who gave me this baggage in the first place!"

At some point, though, we will have to deal with this huge weight on our shoulders. It is a tough choice to say, "I don't want to carry it any longer" and "I am going to get rid of it", but the benefits are huge.

We will be the losers if we do not forgive. Feelings of anger, desire for retribution, and self-pity do not hurt the person they're directed at. As the saying goes, it's like drinking poison and hoping that the other person will die. Our ex is often completely unaware of these feelings. Instead, they hurt us, as well as others close to us, such as our children, our friends, and our wider family.

Recently I read a story with this headline: "Mum: I forgive my ex for blowing me up in car". Victoria Fabian suffered terrible injuries when a booby-trap device blew up her car in March 2010. She said this:

I have forgiven him. I feel too much hatred and anger is only going to bring me down and it's an energy that I don't want to carry around with me... otherwise I would be very bitter and twisted.

The Sun newspaper, 13 February 2012

Archbishop Desmond Tutu, chairman of South Africa's Truth and Reconciliation Commission, confirmed this when he said: "To forgive is not just to be altruistic. It is the best form of self-interest" (The Forgiveness Project, www.theforgivenessproject. com/stories/desmond-tutu).

It is the best thing for us and it is also the best thing for the people around us, such as our children. It is worth recognizing here that, just as we suffer if we do not forgive, so our children will suffer if they are unable to forgive those who have hurt them. If their parents don't forgive each other, it's much harder for children to let go and forgive their parents for the impact on their lives. Children often copy their parents and will be enabled to forgive if their parents show them the way.

What's the benefit?

So, what is the benefit of forgiving? Let me tell you about my experience.

I went through a huge amount of pain and anguish when the news of Karen's affair came out. I had many mixed emotions and I often wondered if she would just come to her senses and come back.

A few months later, when Karen was pushing for a divorce, there came a point when I wanted to see her just so I could tell her how much distress she had caused me, particularly as she had never said sorry for what happened (and has still not done so). She agreed to see me, and before we met I made a list of all the ways she had hurt me: the hurtful experiences, her lies and deception, her broken promises, and all my unfulfilled expectations. It was a long list and was horrible to write because each line was full of pain.

We arranged to meet in a pub on a Monday night and I went to church on the Sunday before. I'd never really thought about forgiveness, as the timing had never been right for me. On that Sunday, for some reason, I found myself being prayed for and I sensed how far short of God's expectation my life was. God has high expectations and I am far from perfect, but I felt his love and forgiveness for me.

After a while my thoughts turned to Karen. I knew that there were various areas where I could have been a better husband. There were issues that I wished we had worked harder at, things that I should have followed up but had left undone. In the light of my own inadequacies and how much I had been forgiven, it was impossible not to forgive her for what she had done. So I forgave Karen. I felt so much better! I felt lightness in my body straight away.

The next day, before I went to meet Karen, I took the list out and looked at it again – just to do some last-minute revising to make sure that I remembered everything! But I was surprised to find that the pain, hurt, and frustration that had accompanied each item on the list had completely gone. As I read each point, I no longer sensed the pain associated with it. I met Karen and although we did discuss some of the points in general, I didn't feel the need to go through the list item by item.

It was a big moment for me, when the hurt left me. My physical life changed as a result of forgiveness – things such as the cloud of blackness that had enveloped me from time to time did not come back. The burden of baggage that I had felt on my shoulders was lifted off. It enabled me to let go of the pain and hurt that had affected my life in so many ways.

I also realized that forgiveness is a continual process. I used to drive past places that brought back painful memories where the hurt would come back and haunt me. Places such as the snooker centre where I had first been introduced to Karen's "friend" Tim; the house where they had been found together by his fiancée; the watch shop where Karen and Tim had chosen a birthday present for me – with "I love you" engraved on the back. Each time these thoughts came back, I had to forgive Karen again. Initially, this happened daily, then weekly, and subsequently less frequently still.

Each time we choose to forgive, the memories have less and less of a hold on us. Over time, I have won the battle with the memories. The scars are there, much like the scars from my medical operations, but there is no pain associated with them. I have been able to start my life afresh. For me, forgiveness was the key to having a future and being free of the past.

Having highlighted why forgiveness helps, let's be clear about what it is and what it is not.

What forgiveness is not

- **Forgiveness is not condoning bad behaviour**
  What the perpetrator did was wrong – forgiveness does not change that.

- **Forgiveness is not denying justice**
  We are not letting them off the hook. Forgiveness means recognizing that *we* ourselves can't decree and deliver justice.

- **Forgiveness is not denying that the hurt happened**
  Forgiveness recognizes the hurt but chooses to let it go.

- **Forgiveness is not demanding an apology**
  Someone saying sorry certainly makes forgiveness much easier, but the person may never apologize. Forgiveness allows us total freedom, regardless of their response.

- **Forgiveness is not pretending that the issue does not matter**

  The issue is important, but we can move on from it. Michael Counsell, whose child was killed by a drunk driver, said this:

  I forgive you does not mean that what you have done does not matter. Forgiveness is a determination to move on from the past, because compassion is better than bitterness.

  The Times newspaper, March 2006

- **Forgiveness is not demanding that the other person change**

  We can never force someone to change.

- **Forgiveness is not allowing ourselves to be taken advantage of or hurt again**

  We need to put appropriate boundaries in place (as discussed in Chapter 3). There is a natural fear that if we forgive someone, we are opening ourselves up to further pain. Forgiveness is not about our being "walked all over again" and becoming a doormat.

- **Forgiveness is not weakness**

  Forgiveness is the brave option.

Mahatma Gandhi said,

The weak can never forgive. Forgiveness is the attribute of the strong.
An Autobiography: The Story of My Experiments with Truth
(CreateSpace Independent Publishing Platform, July 2011)

So what *is* forgiveness?

It's vital to know what forgiveness is *not*, but now let us look in a little more detail at what forgiveness *is*. Here are two very useful definitions. Forgiveness means:

- **Choosing to release someone from punishment; and**
- **Ceasing to hold it against them.**

These meanings are taken from the courtroom. In the first definition, choosing to release someone from punishment, the picture is of us as judge. The accused is found guilty, but we choose to let them go.

In the second definition, ceasing to hold it against them, the picture is of us as victim. Instead of looking for revenge or moral justice, we choose to leave the offence behind us and stop holding it against the perpetrator.

These two actions entail turning away from the event and moving on. This means stopping looking at or thinking about the incident in our mind and focusing on something else in future.

People find the illustration below helpful in this process. In marriage, as in all relationships, if someone does something wrong, the other partner marks it down on an imaginary scorecard. If this board represents my scorecard with Karen, then through normal life there would be a mixture of daily or weekly grievances that we would mark down against each other.

When Karen had her affair, these mounted up.

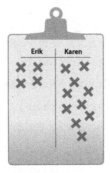

And mounted up further…

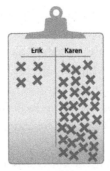

Forgiveness means releasing someone from the punishment implied by that scorecard. It wipes the slate clean. It refuses to hold these wrongs against them in the future. That's what I did with Karen – I wiped her side of the slate clean.

Forgiveness for others, not just your ex

All our relationships will have a scorecard like this. Most of them will have only minor marks, which will be very easy to clean off, and we may not even notice these scorecards. However, other relationships will have major markings on their card, maybe in respect of family members, friends, or other people who have had a negative impact on your life. The same process of forgiveness can be completed with these people, so that you can be released from past hurts.

The author Russ Parker tells the story of a couple who came to him as a result of their plans to divorce. He talks about how he worked with the wife, who had been struggling with some issues related to her father, which had started when she was a child. This is what he writes:

> She had a deep self-loathing, as well as a lot of repressed anger towards her father which she had never voiced. During one of the counselling sessions, she poured out all of the anger that she had previously never mentioned. It was as if the little girl had been locked up inside her and was now free to tell her story. Once the hurt and anger had been let out, she was able to forgive her father and let go of the bitterness she'd had towards him for over thirty years. The result of the experience was that she literally "came back to life.. The lethargy and lack of energy, characteristic of her life, simply disappeared and she rediscovered her capacity for joy and warmth. Her husband reported that he had a new marriage and all plans for divorce were cancelled.
>
> From *Forgiveness is Healing* by Russ Parker (SPCK, 2011)

It is never too late to forgive someone who has had an impact on our life. We can choose to do it whenever we like.

My understanding of the releasing power of forgiveness was initiated by my experience of my spiritual scorecard with God, in which my slate in relationship to God was wiped clean. I am grateful to the author R. T. Kendall, who has written three excellent books on forgiveness. His book Totally Forgiving God *(Hodder & Stoughton, 2012), explores the challenging concept of our need to forgive God where we feel he has let us down and is helpful to those who feel particularly stuck on this issue.*

Forgiveness is a highly effective tool in other relationships, irrespective of your faith or beliefs. Therefore I would encourage everyone to try it out and see what difference it can make.

Forgiveness in hard places

It is important to recognize that this subject is difficult and challenging – it's a hard path. We often get feedback from participants on Restored Lives that forgiveness was both the most important thing they learned on the course and the most difficult. The reason for this is that we have to let go of something that has affected our life significantly. It's always costly to forgive: we sacrifice our desire for justice, our pride, our self-pity, or our guilt and shame. And yet we come out with something much greater – our own freedom and renewed joy – so be bold and courageous as you venture down this path.

I want to reassure you that many people have been through some horrendous relationship breakdowns and gained the freedom that comes through forgiveness. As well as this, people have experienced some of the worst atrocities that life and the world can throw at them yet have still found a power and freedom in ceasing to punish people and not holding it against them.

The actress Emma Thompson said this:

I have spent time with people in Chile and in Argentina whose families were murdered and tortured during the troubled histories of these countries. I have never heard a single one desire revenge. There is no more important undertaking than forgiveness... It is the most powerful weapon we have against terrorism and atrocity.

The Forgiveness Project, www.theforgivenessproject.com

Other stories of forgiveness in hard places stand out, such as that of Corrie ten Boom, who survived Hitler's Ravensbrück concentration camp during the Second World War but lost her sister there. She said this in her book *He Sets the Captive Free* (Kingsway, 1978):

Forgiveness is the key which unlocks the door of resentment and the handcuffs of hatred. It is the power that breaks the chains of bitterness and the shackles of selfishness. What a liberation it is when you can forgive.

Then there are stories from modern-day atrocities such as in Rwanda, where over a million people were massacred in an appalling act of genocide. Bishop John Rucyahana in *The Bishop of Rwanda* (Thomas Nelson, 2008) said this:

I've seen people forgive those who killed their loved ones. I've watched survivors and perpetrators cry together and hug each other through their tears.

A story from Philip Yancey's book *Rumours of Another World* sheds more light on this difficult topic:

Nelson Mandela taught the world a lesson in grace when, after emerging from prison after twenty-seven years and being elected president of South Africa, he asked his jailer to join him on the inauguration platform. He then appointed Archbishop Desmond Tutu to head an official government panel with a daunting name, the Truth and Reconciliation Commission. Mandela sought to defuse the natural pattern of revenge that he had seen in so many countries where one oppressed race or tribe took control from another.

For the next two-and-a-half years, South Africa listened to reports of atrocities coming out of the TRC hearings. The rules were simple: if a white policeman or army officer voluntarily faced his accusers, confessed his crime, and fully acknowledged his guilt, he could not be tried and punished for that crime. Hard-liners grumbled about the obvious injustice of letting criminals go free, but Mandela insisted that the country needed healing even more than it needed justice.

At one hearing, a policeman named van de Broek recounted an incident when he and other officers shot an eighteen-year-old boy and burned the body, turning it on the fire like a piece of barbecue meat in order to destroy the evidence. Eight years later van de Broek returned to the same house and seized the boy's father. The wife was forced to watch as policeman bound her husband on a woodpile, poured gasoline over his body, and ignited it.

The courtroom grew hushed as the elderly woman who had lost first her son and then her husband was given a chance to respond. "What do you want from Mr. van de Broek?" the judge asked. She said she wanted van de Broek to go to the place where they burned her husband's body and gather up the dust so she could give him a decent burial. His head down, the policeman nodded his agreement.

Then she added a further request: "Mr. van de Broek took all my family away from me, and I still have a lot of love to give. Twice a month, I would like for him to come to the ghetto and spend a day with me so I can be a mother to him. And I would like Mr. van de Broek to know that he is forgiven by God, and that I forgive him too. I would like to embrace him so he can know my forgiveness is real."

Spontaneously, some in the courtroom began singing "Amazing Grace" as the elderly woman made her way to the witness stand, but van de Broek did not hear the hymn. He had fainted, overwhelmed.

Philip Yancey, *Rumours of Another World*

These powerful stories from horrendous circumstances show that forgiveness *is* possible, whatever someone may have done to us. Like the elderly woman in South Africa who lost everyone close to her, or Jo Berry who lost her father in the Brighton bombing, we too can choose this route: choose not to punish and not to hold it against them, thus releasing ourselves from the anger and hurt that has arisen. There is a cost to us as we lay down justice and self-pity, but we come out with something much greater – freedom.

The big question now is, how do we do it? I will cover that in the next chapter.

Jodie

I met Edward and we began living together, although we never married. I was running my own business, felt highly capable, and was enjoying being a career woman. Edward had been married before and was something of a workaholic. He had one child from his marriage, whom he idolized, so I felt sure that he would be a marvellous father. We had an easy relationship and never really argued.

I fell pregnant two years later, and Kate was born. I immediately bonded very deeply with her and naturally felt very maternal. When she was six weeks old, Edward announced that he was leaving us. He had already emptied his cupboards. He walked out and we did not see him for seven months. When Kate was around nine months old I felt stressed and was not coping at all well. I began to realize that I was suffering from depression but I was desperate to breastfeed and so would not contemplate taking any form of medication to help with the illness. I found it difficult to mix with other new mothers as I felt the stigma of having been left.

Edward came back for a trial reconciliation that summer but it did not work out. My depression did not lift and I think he found that very hard, as he didn't know how to cope with me. After we had been together for four months, he abruptly left again.

I was supposed to be working as a self-employed person but I was not managing to do anything, nor was I managing to care for Kate. I did go on medication but by then I was very low. My family were overseas and, as I had shut myself away, I had no support network. I became very isolated and came to convince myself that Kate would be better off without me. I attempted suicide and was admitted to a psychiatric hospital. Edward had to move back into our flat for a while to care for Kate.

When I was released from hospital, I was heavily drugged. My bond with Kate had broken down and I felt very detached from her and unable to cope. I had a marvellous doctor, who used to see me every week and give me only a week's medication at a time. I also had regular meetings with the health visitor, who removed all other medication from the flat. Apart from this, and necessary trips to the supermarket, I saw nobody and never went out. Many weeks would pass without my even opening the curtains. Brushing my teeth and putting on an old grey tracksuit was almost more than I could manage.

I had financial pressures, as I lived on benefits. I could not cope with opening the post and so did not pay the bills, and at one point the bailiffs came round. At the same time I was also being stressed by trying to get some sort of support for Kate from Edward. His rejection of me felt hard enough, but I found his rejection of our daughter even more painful: he never came to see Kate.

After I had been living in isolation for about eighteen months, a friend told me about Restored Lives. It took me a long time to make the effort to ring, but eventually I did and I enrolled on the course. It was a huge step to come on the course and even getting there that first night was really hard. But I haven't looked back since, and am really glad I made it.

Tell us about your experience of forgiveness.

Until I got on the course, it was zero. I'd heard all about forgiveness because I went to a convent school, but I wasn't practising any of those things in my life at the time. When I went on the course I was in pretty bad shape, and a lot of it went over my head. I think I just sat there in a fairly comatose state for most of it, but I kept the notes and all the people were so lovely that I thought that I would do an Alpha Course.

That changed my life, because I became a Christian and received God's forgiveness for me. As a result, I thought that I had better go back and read the Restored Lives notes again. That's when I began to look at what forgiveness is. At the time I was still feeling the pain, the hurt, the suffering, and the disappointment and it was keeping me almost a prisoner in my own body.

I felt that I had to forgive Edward for everything that had gone on, but it wasn't an easy thing. I didn't wake up one morning and think, "OK, it's forgiveness day today, and off we go!" I had to work on it. I thought about it a lot and eventually I thought, "I'm just going to say these words and hope that I start to mean it."

I did, and it was a real turning point in my life. I changed. It changed the way I feel about myself, and what I felt about Edward and what he'd done wrong. I had built up a fairy-tale existence in my mind: nice job, lovely partner, good lifestyle, etc., and the break-up of our relationship caused it to tumble down around me. I was standing in the ruins of my own castle and it was like a prison. I had to forgive to break out of that prison, break through the rubble, and get out into the big wide world.

Forgiveness is like peeling away the layers of an onion. The hardest part is getting the skin off the first layer, which is like the first *time you forgive. Then there are still little things you have to forgive – I still have to forgive Edward regularly for minor hurts when they happen, but they're not as bad as the huge things. I don't go home weeping any more when something happens or when my daughter says something about her dad. It hurts, I hurt for her, but I forgive him and, in forgiving him, it stops it hurting me. It takes the pain away and I don't hurt any more. I'm so thankful for that and I'm so grateful to have this amazing key in my hand that's forgiveness, and to be able just to unlock the door every time I need to.*

My depression lifted and I went back to work when Kate was four. My relationship with her was also restored. I had moved into a time of giving rather than receiving. Looking back, I am sure that the medication I took for the depression was also a key part of my recovery. It enabled me to function from day to day, and that opened the way for healing.

I am now really excited about my future. I am about to train as a teacher and I am moving forward with great hope.

TOOLBOX TO TAKE AWAY
Freedom from the past

Forgiveness enables you to let go of the pain and hurt that have arisen in the past

Forgiveness is one of the most misunderstood concepts today

Forgiveness is available to everyone, regardless of their religious beliefs

Two reasons to forgive:

- *Revenge doesn't work.*
- *We lose out if we don't forgive.*

Forgiveness is not about:

- *condoning bad behaviour;*
- *denying justice;*
- *denying that the hurt happened;*
- *demanding an apology;*
- *pretending that the issue does not matter;*
- *demanding that the other person change;*
- *allowing ourselves to be taken advantage of or hurt again;*
- *weakness.*

Forgiveness is about:

- *wiping the marks off the scorecard;*
- *it means:*
  - **choosing to release someone from punishment**
  - **ceasing to hold it against them;**
- *keeping on forgiving day after day.*

Chapter 6

How to let go

I loved being with this other woman; I loved the fun we had. So I made the choice to divorce, convinced that I could keep a close relationship with the girls – it was such a huge mistake… If there is any good in this story it is that I went and apologized to my wife. I said sorry to Phoebe and also to the girls for the pain that I had caused. She has been very gracious and we now have a very good relationship, probably much better than before.

Joe

You may be living through a period in which you "can't think about letting go now". Others may have read the last chapter on "Freedom from the past" and decided that you do not want to forgive. If you are in either of these two situations, I want to say thank you for reading up to this point. It is vital that you should be free to come to your own conclusions and that everyone's views and choices should be respected in these fundamental matters.

Others of you may want to investigate the subject further, or may already be thinking that the cost of letting go is an attractive price to pay to be rid of the pain of the past. In this situation, it's common to ask the question: "Yes, but how?" For this reason I have outlined four practical steps to enable you to implement it in your life.

Some people find forgiveness relatively easy and, if you are one of them, the steps in this chapter will just give colour to your natural choice. However, many others will use the steps as the "science" behind each choice, which will strengthen your resolve to keep going and guide you along what is often a challenging path.

I have separated the steps for "forgiving others" from those for "forgiveness for ourselves" because, although the steps are exactly the same, the focus and perspective are slightly different. You may feel that you fit into only one of these categories, but I would encourage you to work through both processes. You may indeed be the victim in your relationship breakdown, but, as a tool for life, forgiving yourself is critical to having a healthy future. As well as that, many people feel they have carried out right and wrong actions in their relationships – a quote from the author Alexander Solzhenitsyn sums up this broad point:

> *If only there were evil people somewhere insidiously committing evil deeds and it were necessary only to separate them from the rest of us and destroy them. But the line dividing good and evil cuts through the heart of every human being, and who is willing to destroy a piece of his own heart?*

This story from John also highlights the point:

> *I found out that Sarah was having an affair and realized that our life and our family were about to fall apart. I felt devastated that Sarah had slept with another man, I found it very difficult to know how to interact with her physically, and we never slept with each other again.*
> *My main emotion was anger, and I kept relentlessly questioning her about why she had done this. I had regular waves of red-mist*

anger towards the other man. I wanted to contact his wife and son to make them aware of what he had done.

I now see how I laid the foundations of the ultimate breakdown in the marriage. I started a business with a good friend and it went from strength to strength. We moved to bigger and bigger houses – the cars, the holidays – everything went up a gear and we were "living the dream". I provided all I could for Sarah and our two boys – everything, that is, apart from me. Naively, I thought that, if I provided all the material things anyone could want in life, Sarah would be happy.

Then came the biggest statement of our success, a motor yacht. Weekends were spent in Spain living the high life, often with business colleagues and not with Sarah. Looking back, I realized I too had been having an affair, but my affair was with the yacht and the lifestyle that came with it. I was totally overwhelmed with guilt for the part I had played in disengaging from Sarah. I therefore had to forgive myself as well as Sarah. I now realize that forgiving myself and her would release me and take away all that anger.

I reflect on how far I have come and my dream of a most amicable divorce is almost a reality, although it has taken a long time and a lot of hard work. I think the reason for improvement is forgiveness. It was, and continues to be, the foundation for moving on. It is still very painful, being away from the boys for so much of the time, and I have to forgive Sarah all over again whenever I feel myself getting angry over not being with her and the boys.

Blocks to forgiveness

Before we look through the steps we need to take to achieve forgiveness, it might be helpful to review some of the blocks that can prevent us from letting go.

Self-pity

You may find it difficult to forgive because you have, whether intentionally or unintentionally, actually come to enjoy feeling like a victim. Being the victim increases the sympathy you receive from others and makes you feel better – it makes you feel justified and valued. You may not want to forgive because you fear you will lose this support and that it will remove your sense of being "right".

> I remember one person who was in a state of severe self-pity many years after her legal divorce had come through. For months, every time she spoke to me she referred to her ex's past wrongdoings, and she was finding it very difficult to move on.

Focusing actively on the past fixes you in the past. Forgiveness does not change who was right or wrong, but it breaks the pattern of holding things against someone and allows you to take responsibility for your future.

To maintain power over your ex

You may want to try to keep some power over your ex, to give you extra "moral high ground" or additional negotiating power. For example you may say to yourself: "You have hurt me so much that you owe me a big financial settlement." Maybe you feel that you will not get as good a deal in your finances or your child's contact arrangements if you forgive your ex.

However, I have seen people forgive their ex at the beginning or even in the middle of a difficult legal battle, which has made the resolution of their dispute easier and better. Their experience has been that forgiveness has removed their bitterness and given them the freedom to make good choices in the legal battle, helping their self-confidence as well as their future relationship.

This benefit occurs because you are not trying to punish your ex through the divorce process or gain revenge. Trying to gain some form of revenge or compensation through a court process usually just increases the cost and stress.

Not being good enough

We all make mistakes in life, but some people have a recording in their head which repeats over and over again the message that they have failed and are not good enough. This is a significant block to forgiving yourself as well as to forgiving others, because you expect the same, unreasonably high standards from both you and them.

The messages in your mind will have arisen for various different reasons and will run along the following lines:

I must always fix problems / have a clean house / look nice / have good children

I should be nicer / thinner / funnier / married

I must never argue / be angry / be quiet

I'm not clever enough / helpful enough / talented enough

Feelings of shame, passed to us by our families and friends, may be at the root of these emotions (see Chapter 2 – Understanding the emotional impact).

This is a pattern of thinking and behaving that can be recognized and changed, thus releasing the ability to forgive both yourself and others.

To protect yourself from the risk of it happening again

Some people want to keep their feelings of pain very close to their heart and mind, as it gives them a sense of protection. You think that focusing on the pain will remind you of the event so that you can stop it from ever happening to you again. You will fear that forgetting the event and the pain it caused might allow your ex or someone else to do it again in the future.

But, sadly, when you sharpen your focus on the source of the pain you hurt yourself more and become further dented by its impact on your life. The reverse is better – let go of the pain and then ensure that you have the right boundaries in place to prevent it from happening again.

Jumping ahead too quickly

Some people are very good at focusing on the next goal and avoiding brooding on the past. Throwing ourselves into our work, our family or another pursuit can fill our time, thereby evading any thoughts of the past and giving us a sense of moving on.

> I remember one person who felt that she was well over her break-up and had just started a new relationship. She said, "I've moved on completely so there is no need to forgive." She was a friendly person, but when she mentioned her ex her tone became uncharacteristically spiteful, and you could see that there was still an emotional landmine inside her.

Painful feelings that are not dealt with are buried like landmines ready to threaten your future relationships.

Forgiving frees you from worrying about mentioning your ex or having any fear of meeting him/her again. A good test of your own freedom is the ability to look back and talk about your ex or past events without the pain and the hurt hitting you. If your emotions tend to boil up when you talk about past events or you feel a substantial fear of meeting them, then forgiveness will help you.

1. Forgiving others

There are four steps to forgiving others:

Step 1: Accept what has happened and the hurt it has caused

You have to be honest with yourself and accept both what has happened to you and the hurt caused by those events. It is all too easy to deny these thoughts and feelings, and even to refuse to accept that the situation is really happening.

Often the shock of bad news will paralyse your mind, possibly for a very long time. Sometimes the cruel or abusive behaviour has become so regular that you no longer know what is normal or appropriate. Some people get lost in a dream that things will go back to normal.

Annie mentioned this acceptance stage in her story in Chapter 2: "the beginning of the process of recovery was acceptance". Accepting that the events have really happened and recognizing the pain associated with them is a vital start to recovery.

Be honest about your feelings: who has hurt you? There may be people other than your ex who have caused you pain – perhaps friends and family members.

Some people find it helpful to make a list of their hurts and a list of the people who have caused them.

Personal exercise

Write down the names of those who have caused you pain and hurt.

Step 2: Acknowledge responsibility

It's relatively easy to acknowledge responsibility when it's clear who is at fault. For example, when one person becomes mentally ill and abusive, or where a person is an addict. It is important to recognize these situations.

However, relationships are rarely black and white and are made up of a multitude of actions and behaviours, causing differing reactions and responses. Some of our responses will be healthy and some will cause further division. It's therefore unusual for there to be only one person to blame when things go wrong, which makes it difficult to work out individual responsibility in a relationship breakdown.

Obviously some choices are much worse than others, and these may lead to primary responsibility. But it's common for both parties to have either aggravated the situation or left things undone over a period of time, and this may imply responsibility from both parties.

Whatever has happened to us, we need to be ready to acknowledge our own contribution to the breakdown of the relationship and the situation we are now in, however small it may be, as this will help us to let go. If you feel as though you are purely the victim, I urge you to think about whether you contributed in any way to the difficulties in the relationship.

For me, it was strangely helpful to realize that I had not been the perfect husband to Karen. I look back and see that there were a couple of important areas which I should have been much more proactive to resolve. However, sorting it out always seemed too difficult. Obviously there is a massive difference in the consequences of different actions, but recognizing my own poor choices or lack of effort helped me to forgive her for hers.

It is important to stand back and take a sensible, overall view of responsibility. We must recognize major actions and their consequences, but we must not focus solely on them. We should also consider other choices and actions made over a longer period.

Personal exercise

Where do you feel the responsibility lies in your situation?

Step 3: Choose to release

If you recognize that someone has hurt you then the next step in forgiveness is to choose to release. This bit can be tough. You need to decide to do two things:

1. Stop punishing the person; and

2. Stop holding the event and the hurt against that person.

Sometimes the thing they did may be huge, such as addiction, abuse, or adultery. If this feels too big for you to let go of, then start small. It reminds me of the old joke: "How do you eat an elephant?" Answer: "One bite at a time."

Start small – try to forgive a different person who has done something minor to you. Then forgive your ex for something petty that irritates you – maybe their rude attitude on the phone, or being annoying about dividing possessions. You will begin to feel the difference that it makes and you can then try it with the bigger issues.

Some people have found that they would like to say "I forgive you" face to face, although you need to think carefully about whether this is appropriate in your particular situation. It is good to write down your process of forgiveness in a journal or in a letter that you may or may not send.

Whether you tell the person or not doesn't matter here. Nor is it important that the person really understands the situation from your perspective. The person you are forgiving may not say sorry and may not even think that they have done anything wrong. The important part to remember is that *you* are in control here; *you* have the option to forgive and become free *irrespective* of whether they apologize or recognize their error.

This is the exciting point, because you have control. Sometimes a divorce makes those involved feel quite out of control of events, but here you are in control of whether you carry the bitterness into the future. In addition, being a choice, it is not necessary for you to "feel" that you want to do it – quite often, taking an active step enables the positive feelings to follow on behind. The important point is that it's your choice to be free from these issues.

Personal exercise

Visualize in your mind (or physically make) a scorecard, representing your relationship with the other person, on a blackboard, a whiteboard, or even just a plain piece of paper, with a light-marking pencil and rubber.

Mark up with crosses the painful issues on their side of the scorecard – maybe even acknowledging each hurt as you do so.

Then make an active choice and wipe each cross out, saying, "I stop punishing you for this. I cease to hold it against you."

Then, once you have erased all the crosses on their side, fill in the sentence below and say it out loud:

"I choose to forgive _____
for the breakdown in our relationship. I release

_____

from my punishment and I cease to hold it against them in the future."

Step 4: Make forgiveness an ongoing choice

We then have to go on releasing – or forgiving – again and again. I had to forgive Karen most days and often more than once each day. Sometimes I found it difficult and at other times it was easier.

Forgiveness is not just a one-off event; it's a continuing process that gets a bit easier each time we choose to do it. Each time we reiterate our forgiveness, we confirm our first act of forgiving someone. This is where we need to be strong and courageous, especially when there is an ongoing relationship with an ex.

Personal exercise

Whenever negative thoughts come back into your mind,
read out the sentence given above in Step 3.

2. Forgiveness for ourselves

It is healthy to consider any crosses on your side and to seek forgiveness for your own actions. As we look at this topic it's useful to reflect on the range of issues that could be included here. For ease of reference I have split them into *small crosses* and *big crosses*.

Small crosses

This is Pietro's story regarding some of his "small crosses":

Many years after our separation, thanks to the encouragement of some friends, I felt that I needed to ask forgiveness from my wife. Yes, just for me, not her. Forgiveness for the fact that I had thought I had no responsibility for what happened. Forgiveness for my faults that I had never recognized before.

Like many separated parents, we used to meet in a "neutral zone", and this time I asked for her forgiveness. She was not expecting that. It was not the usual exchange of information about our son, the alternating weekends or school scores – the subjects that normally filled most of our dialogues. She listened in silence to my request for forgiveness, with her eyes a little bit watery.

The next day, she sent me three long text messages. Words that I will always carry in my heart, which are part of our love story, which surmount the barriers of time and cannot be changed.

I don't know how far I have travelled, but I realize that before that moment I could not look at a couple embracing or in an attitude of tenderness without feeling pain and perhaps envy. Instead, now, I

am happy that they make a beautiful family and pray that their love
will never end, that they will always be together!

Pietro's story highlights the amazing release that comes from getting rid of even the small crosses.

Big crosses

Some of our choices and actions can have significant consequences, and when this causes real hurt we end up with a big cross on our side of the scorecard. These can be very difficult to deal with because the pain caused can be substantial.

I have heard many people say "I can forgive others but I can't forgive myself", and I remember one person saying, "I know that God forgives me but I can't let it go." These feelings of guilt can be crippling and can dog us for years.

In the same way that not forgiving someone poisons us, not forgiving ourselves will also poison us and stop us moving successfully forward.

The good news is that there is a solution for both small and big crosses and it is the same path as for forgiving others.

Step 1: Accept what's happened and the hurt it has caused

The first step is to accept and recognize what's happened and the hurt that you have caused.

Try to pinpoint the exact cause of any guilt rather than wallow in a general feeling of being to blame. Feelings of guilt arise when our actions fail to meet either our own or someone else's expectations or standards. Guilt is a natural response at these moments, especially when we know we have hurt or caused a loss to someone else. Being specific about these events will help clarify emotions in our minds.

Personal exercise

Write down here the names of those whom you have hurt,
and how.

Step 2: Acknowledge responsibility

You need to acknowledge responsibility for how you have acted
and recognize the impact of your choices on other people.

Discussing the situation with someone else is very helpful,
as it clarifies the issues in your mind and allows you to be
honest with yourself. If you are wary of speaking with a friend,
then find a counsellor or a church leader who can listen to you.

Saying sorry

Saying sorry is not the same as forgiving. "Sorry" acknowledges
responsibility for our words and actions and recognizes their
impact on someone else. "Sorry" acts like the handle on the
door of forgiveness. This handle helps the door to be opened
to remove the barrier between two people.

A genuine apology validates the pain felt by the other
person and gives them an opportunity to forgive in return.
Saying "Sorry, will you forgive me?" to someone therefore
becomes a very powerful step in the process of resolving
conflict.

But being brave enough to say these words may not
immediately result in harmony. It can take time for them
to sink in. They might even be met with further anger and
another discussion on the pain and the hurt that you have
caused. So think carefully about how and when this is to be
done. However, I have always seen these words as productive
for the person saying sorry, and often for both people. An
apology will often lead to a very healthy discussion between

a separating couple, and is a positive step in the process of moving on for both people.

> Health warning: An apology needs to be genuine and clear. Benjamin Franklin said, "Never ruin an apology with an excuse." Don't justify your actions after the apology, such as by saying "sorry, but..." as it only opens the wound once again; just say sorry and recognize the impact on the other person.

Willingness to make amends

In theory, following an apology, we should seek to "make amends" for past actions or, if there is an ongoing relationship, seek to adapt our future behaviour should the same circumstances arise. If we have stolen money, it's clear that making amends would mean returning the funds. However, in relationships, making amends can be very difficult, particularly in cases of severe physical or mental abuse.

> Please note: This process of acknowledging responsibility is NOT about trying to weigh us all down with guilt. Similarly, we can argue for ages about whether guilt is right or wrong in any given situation. The important point here is recognizing what we are thinking and feeling and, if we have a sense of guilt, doing something about it.

Personal exercise

Which actions can you take responsibility for? How can you apologize for them?

Step 3: Choose to release

Once you have acknowledged your actions and apologized, you can seek release. This process can be greatly assisted by speaking with the person concerned (even if it's your ex), as this sets up a real milestone, although you should sense-check this approach to ensure that it is appropriate in your situation.

There are three scorecards that are helpful to think through:

i. The scorecard with the person you have hurt

The scorecard with the person you have hurt has marks on your side of the line. Acknowledging your actions, saying sorry, and asking, for example, your ex to forgive you is the remedy for removing these marks.

How your ex responds to you is now in their hands. Your ex may or may not choose to forgive you but that is not something that you can dictate. You have done everything in your power to clear the marks from the scorecard, which is an important landmark for you and an action that should be greatly respected.

Some people find it extremely hard to forgive others (the less you have experienced forgiveness yourself, the harder it is to forgive), so be patient with your ex and be willing to apologize more than once so that they know you mean it.

Apologizing and doing all that you can to seek forgiveness gives them the best opportunity to let go of the pain that they have experienced. This is also the key step for you, which allows you to move on successfully.

ii. The scorecard with yourself

An often overlooked scorecard, but vitally important, is the one that you hold against yourself. This is where you have your own standard of conduct or desired outcome and, if you fail to live up to this, you mark it down against yourself.

Having acknowledged your mistake and accepted the situation, you need to remove the marks against yourself. You can do this however much your mind says something is "unforgiveable" – it isn't; you can forgive yourself and let go of those crosses.

iii. The scorecard with God

I found it important to say sorry and seek forgiveness for my actions from God, and I know of many other people who have had a similar experience. This process also gave me a deeper understanding of the issues surrounding forgiveness and letting go.

The result of going through all three scorecards is that we choose to stop punishing and stop holding the hurt against ourselves.

Personal exercise

This is a moment when you can choose to release yourself.
Visualize or create and mark up three different scorecards:

1. *With your ex: think through how and when you can say sorry to them.*

2. *With yourself: mark up the situations in which you have failed to live up to your own standards. Then choose to clean your own scorecard. Then read out the sentence below:*

   "I choose to forgive myself for the breakdown in our relationship. I cease to hold it against myself and I release myself from punishment."

3. *With God: apologize to God and ask for forgiveness. You may want to speak with a church leader, but know that you are forgiven.*

Step 4: Make forgiveness an ongoing choice

Each time a situation or a feeling of guilt comes to mind, you need to go through the same process of forgiving yourself. You may need to repeat this process again and again to yourself or to others.

This is a choice, day after day, which is vital and gets much easier each time you do it.

Personal exercise

Work through Steps 2 and 3 whenever the feelings of guilt come back into your mind.

Take your time, but be brave

Take your time and test out the benefits of forgiveness. Some people find that it is a slow process of working through each step. Sometimes we recognize our own faults, while at other times we are able to see only those of the other party. We may have been able to say sorry, but then realize later that we could have put it better.

There may be someone who regularly enjoys reminding us of the past and we may need to put a boundary in place so this doesn't keep happening. This process of slowly moving towards forgiveness is normal, especially when there are difficult circumstances and an ongoing relationship involved.

If you are finding this subject difficult I would encourage you, instead of thinking "Can I forgive?", to ask the question "When will I be able to forgive?" Think through which barriers you need to overcome before you can take each step and get to forgiveness.

Forgiveness is ultimately a choice and a process. Test it by first making the choice to do it and then seeing what your feelings are like afterwards. Often we have to be brave and be the **first to forgive** in order to get rid of those landmines inside us and gain release from the pain and hurt. But remember, this is for our benefit – try it out!

Complete forgiveness

The result of working through each of the four stages is that you arrive at a state of genuine and complete forgiveness. You may not be able to contemplate this yet, but I can say that, although it takes time and determination, it bears huge fruit.

Complete forgiveness means that you want the best for the person you have forgiven. You want them to succeed, you want them to have a good life, you encourage them, you want them to have a good relationship with their children, and you wish them well in all that they do.

Don't worry if you can't even imagine this at the moment; just hold on to it as the ultimate goal of complete freedom *for you*. Complete forgiveness creates a vision of what life is like when you completely let go of your painful history.

"Forgive and forget"

I have heard people say that you must forgive *and* forget (with the emphasis on forgetting), but this is not quite right. Forgiveness gives you *the ability* to forget because the event, which is still important, now doesn't have the same emotional triggers.

This situation is similar to when a doctor says you are better but you still need time to get used to your healing. For example, I broke my knee cap once, the doctors reconstructed it back together. They said, "it's fixed" (that's the moment of forgiveness), but then I still required months of physical work to strengthen the muscles and learn how to walk again. After a long and persistent process, I was able to run around without pain and now all that's left is a scar (that's when you are able to forget).

Forgetting, in this situation, means not remembering the pain and the hurt that were associated with an episode of your life. For small events in life maybe you can forget, but you can't forget that you were married – however, you can let go of the bitterness that you felt.

The subject of learning from experience to create good boundaries in your future relationships can be very important here, as these boundaries will help to protect you in the future.

Some small examples highlight this: if someone is rude to you on the phone, you might forgive them for being rude but then think about what you might say to them next time to stop it happening again. Or if your ex is seeking an excessive amount of money in the financial settlement, you might forgive them for being selfish but continue to work towards a reasonable settlement with your mediator.

Think carefully through what boundaries you need in the future.

Focus your thoughts on something else

The result of forgiveness is that you naturally let go of the event and become able to focus on something else. This turning away from continually reliving what happened will enable you to focus your attention freely on other activities or new goals in life.

Personal exercise

Go through a checklist of whether you have completely forgiven someone (OK – this is a hard test!):

Do you still talk about the subject?

Does the issue go around your mind like a continuing conversation?

When someone mentions the person, do you get angry or depressed quickly?

Can you speak about your relationship without significant sadness or bitterness?

Can you remember the good times in your relationship?

Do you resent them (or yourself) on account of other problems or consequences in your life?

Can you meet them without those feelings welling up inside you?

Have you wished them (and/or yourself) well in the future?

Keep these in mind throughout your journey as milestones on the path to complete recovery and freedom.

I am convinced that, if we do not forgive, we lose out twice: first for the act committed against us; and second for the effect of holding on to the hatred, pain, and self-pity. If we do forgive, we gain freedom from the past and ensure that our future relationships will not be affected by it – in effect, we recover the ability to make good choices for the future so we can to move on successfully.

Joe
......

I had a fairly normal family life. I was brought up in Manchester in a loving family, and even though my parents separated when I was in my twenties, I always felt that I had a good start in life.

I married Phoebe when I was twenty-seven and we have two beautiful daughters. Our family life and marriage was good – both Phoebe and I both made a big effort to make time for the family.

There were then a few key changes which, when I look back, made a big impact on our lives. Firstly, I started working much more in and around London, where a lot of my work in property and construction was going on. Then, around the same time, my wife's mum died. They were very close to each other and it affected her in ways that looking back surprised us both.

We started having more issues in our marriage and to be honest our sex life disappeared. I say this not as a justification for the biggest mistake in my life, but just to be honest. My biggest mistake was having an affair, but it didn't feel like a mistake at the time – life in London was fun and all my friends and colleagues seemed to be very liberal in their relationships. I started working more closely with one particular colleague and she was really keen on me. In a way she pursued me, but in another way I loved the attention she gave me. It made me feel valued. I resisted for a long time but in the end I succumbed and we had a relationship for about four years.

Things came to a head when the woman started pushing me to make our relationship permanent, and she said that she really wanted to marry and commit fully. I had never thought about leaving my marriage, but over the years my relationship with Phoebe deteriorated, and suddenly the only thing that kept me home were my girls.

Life in London was much more enjoyable and exciting, and I had really fallen in love. I loved being with this other woman, I loved the fun we had. So I made the choice to divorce, convinced that I could keep a close relationship with the girls – it was such a huge mistake.

It was initially difficult and Phoebe was hurt, but we tried to be sensible about things and sorted the legal issues out reasonably well. The real turning point for me came around nine months later. I had made the biggest choice in my life to leave my family to be with "the love of my life" and then suddenly my relationship with this woman changed. She became distracted and then left me.

I couldn't believe it. You may find this difficult to believe but I was so angry and hurt. All the painful things that we talk about at the beginning of the course, I felt. I continued to work but only as a shadow. I was so lost. I had given up everything and then had nothing.

Yes I had done something similar to Phoebe, but that didn't dawn on me for a long time. I was lost in the wilderness and couldn't believe the pain I was going through. Of course I now see very clearly that I had caused so much pain to my wife and then I got it thrown back in my face.

If there is any good in this story it is that I went and apologized to my wife. I said sorry to Phoebe and also to the girls for the pain that I had caused. She has been very gracious and we now have a very good relationship, probably much better than before. We see each other regularly and I've been to stay with her and she's been down to London to stay with me. We actually take care of each other quite a lot these days. Her willingness to forgive and allow a relationship with me is something for which I am deeply grateful.

We see the girls together and we talk about them and chat about

*our lives a lot. It's strange, we communicate really well now. I even
tried to suggest to her a while ago that we should get together again.
She said no; once was enough. She couldn't imagine getting together
again or getting remarried although I was quite prepared to do that.*

TOOLBOX TO TAKE AWAY
How to let go

Check for blocks to forgiveness:

- *self-pity;*
- *power over your ex;*
- *"you're not good enough";*
- *protecting yourself;*
- *jumping ahead too fast.*

Work through the forgiveness steps for others and yourself:

- *Step 1: Accept the hurt.*
- *Step 2: Acknowledge your responsibility.*
- *Step 3: Choose to release – stop punishing and stop holding
  it against them.*
- *Step 4: Make forgiveness an ongoing choice.*

Be the first to forgive

Forgiveness gives you the ability to forget

Seek complete forgiveness to arrive at complete freedom

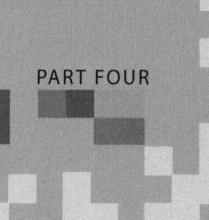

PART FOUR

WHAT HAPPENS TO EVERYONE ELSE?

Chapter 7

Managing other relationships

"Being suddenly single in my thirties meant the whole rhythm of my life changed.... I wanted to be going out in the evenings, meeting new people. They were up to their elbows in nappies and desperate for a good night's sleep.

"Once you get to the point of accepting your new situation and trying to make the best of it you discover there is a world of fun and exciting times out there."

Katie

The earthquake of relationship breakdown affects others around you and you have to be prepared to deal with this. Don't be surprised the shockwaves of your altered circumstances continue to reverberate around you and change your other relationships for a while.

Friendships

I wish that I could say that all your friends will come rallying round you, but this is not always the case. Cards and emails may not come flooding in as they might in the event of bereavement or a major illness, as people are much less sure how to react.

Every friendship you have will be affected by the breakdown. Some may become closer, some may become awkward for a time, and others will disappear completely. These changes will be painful and frustrating.

Put as much effort as you can into maintaining the friendships that you believe are the most important, but don't take it personally if they don't work out as you would like them to – it's part of your changing life.

Normally, the friends that you had before you knew your partner will stay with you; if they start to "side" and spend more time with your ex, however, it can be very difficult to bear. There is little you can do in these situations if they are inclined to show favouritism, but, to make up for it, other friends will become closer.

I made the effort to get back in touch with some old school friends and spend more time with them. I realized that my marriage had dragged me away from them and, although they were a little upset that I had lost touch with them, we quickly made up for lost time and these friendships became a great source of comfort to me.

Trusted friends

You may find that certain people become your closest, "trusted" friends. These are the people who will make more time for you and whom you feel you can confide in over a whole range of topics. These trusted friends should be people whose judgment you respect and who will not be afraid to tell you if you step out of line. It's important to nurture and encourage such friendships, because having this close support through your journey will sustain you.

I was lucky to have a friend who told me from the beginning that he would be happy to support me as I went through the process. I could ring him and know that he would listen. He would regularly call me and ask me how things were going. One of the things I found very helpful was that I allowed him to ask the challenging questions – the ones other friends would find it difficult to ask. This meant that I could be honest with him about my actions and feelings.

Mutual friends

Mutual friendships that you and your ex have developed together are often one of the hardest areas, because there will be divided loyalties. In a sense this is a "no-win" situation, in which your friends will find it incredibly difficult to maintain a close connection to both you and your ex.

Some friends may cause you deep hurt by siding with your ex and possibly doing or saying unkind things in the process. You may have to accept this and forgive them. Be encouraged that these friendships can be rebuilt in time if you want them to.

It is possible to continue to have mutual friends but it's important to have clear boundaries in this area. It's a good idea to refrain from asking friends about your ex, as the information that comes from this is nearly always unhelpful and also puts your friends in an extremely awkward position. You may need to review the access your ex or your ex's friends have to any of your social media websites, such as facebook. It's hard to get used to, but what your ex does now is, more likely than not, nothing to do with you. It is therefore best for all concerned to tell your friends in advance that you don't want updates on your ex's situation.

Social life

Your social life will also change, especially at the beginning, when you may receive fewer invitations from friends who are working out how to handle this change: events or places to which you used to enjoy going can become danger zones of uncertainty and awkwardness. They will bring up memories of the past and you will have to act in a different way from how you did when you went together as a couple.

The first year after a relationship breakdown becomes the year of "first times" – the first Christmas without your family, the first anniversary of your wedding day post-separation, the first New Year's Eve party without your ex, etc. These are hard, and it's therefore good to try to be proactive and plan something different this time. This creates an event to look forward to and stops you thinking about "last year".

Big celebrations and events are often even harder, especially if you find it difficult to talk about the past. You have to face all your extended family and friends and get through the first instance of saying what has happened or responding to simple questions such as "How are you?" Having a standard answer prepared in advance can be helpful. However, there is always the risk of someone asking you how your ex is without knowing that you have split up.

Ten years after I had divorced, someone who didn't know we had split up asked me, "How's Karen?" It wasn't his fault, as he had been away, but you need a standard response to these unfortunate questions otherwise you are caught out each time.

On top of this, you are trying to work out whether you want to go out at all and whom you want to see. This changing social life is painful to come to terms with, but remember that it's got nothing to do with who you are as a person; it's all because your life situation is changing.

For some people, who suddenly find themselves as full time carers for their children with no support, it can be especially difficult. I would encourage you to get as much help and support as you can to give you some time off.

Just say yes; just say no

It can be difficult to change the behaviour of others, but you *can* change your own actions. If you want to go out more and you feel up to it, then give those friends a ring and tell them that you will say yes to any of their, or their friends', invitations.

On the other hand, you are also free to say "no" to invitations you're not comfortable with. Practise the line "Thank you so much but I'm afraid I won't be able to come." No complex excuses are needed!

Often the reality is that you probably need to make judicious use of both of these responses to begin with, until you start to find your feet.

Take up something new

As your friends change and your social life changes, it's vital to make your own choices about how you want to fill your time in the future. Starting something new is a great opportunity, even if it's only a small activity.

One man found Saturdays very hard, as they suddenly seemed so long and empty. He joined a walking club and went on all-day hikes with a large group of people. They didn't get back till 7 pm and by the time he had eaten and had a bath he was ready for bed.

A woman would regularly arrange a babysitter for her three children and go to a nightclub with a friend. They hadn't done this for years, but found that dancing late into the night was uplifting as well as exhausting.

This is what Bill said about his response to this situation:

You've got to be really pragmatic with yourself and say, "This is the situation; I've got to deal with it and not dwell on it." That is sometimes easier said than done, but I would encourage you to find a different and regular focus for you and your energies. Getting involved in something – perhaps a voluntary organization, perhaps a hobby or exercise, something that completely channels your physical and emotional energies, something that challenges you – is really important. It's amazing how focusing your mind in a different direction for a while can liberate you from those bad feelings.

This can be a good time to take up a new hobby or form of exercise. You may not feel like it at first, but making an active choice to start something new is positive in itself. Take time to think about what you enjoy doing and then just go for it. Try to join clubs in a social environment rather than just doing it by yourself: so, if you like running, run with some friends; if it's drawing, join an art club; or if it's cooking, then cook for a school or charitable event.

Going on a relationship breakdown course can also be an opportunity for new friendships to form. People often continue to meet socially after a course has ended, as the continued support of someone who understands your situation can be enormously beneficial.

These new activities will help you to build your self-confidence as well as to find new friends.

Thomas said this:

Ask yourself: what things make you happy and what do you enjoy doing? This is something that I found really positive about my divorce process, because I felt I had forced myself into this contorted shape to try to please my ex. Then during the separation I realized that I didn't know myself at all. I had no idea what I enjoyed doing. I knew I hated R & B music (which was the only thing she listened to), but what music did I enjoy? So I started listening to lots of different music and going to gigs.

I remembered that I'd always wanted to sail, so I went on a thirteen-week course. It was a real slog and I had to work hard, but it took my mind off things. I had wanted to learn to ride a motorbike but had never been allowed to by my ex, so I went and did that too. I even realized that I loved culture and started going to art galleries. I really enjoyed it all, and it was part of finding out who I was.

I know it's easier said than done and you may not feel like it initially, but when you make that decision it is a really positive thing.

Working life

Your working life will also be affected. Your mind will often be preoccupied by what's happening outside the workplace, and you will be easily distracted.

One person said she used to stare at her computer screen for hours on end, going over and over her problems, completely unable to do anything constructive.

If you feel that your performance is being affected, it might be a good idea to tell someone at work so that they understand what you are going through. Most people have either been through separation and divorce themselves or know someone who has, and therefore most of them will be sympathetic to your situation.

Try to keep your workplace free from the ramifications of divorce as much as possible. Banning calls and emails from and to your ex while at work is probably best for both of you.

I know someone whose ex rang her at work to say he was getting married to the woman he'd left her for two months before! You definitely do not need that kind of distraction at the office!

Parents and siblings

Yes – everything is affected, including your relationships with your parents and siblings, as they will be experiencing many different feelings themselves, possibly including shock, guilt, anxiety, and anger.

Your family will have built up a relationship with your ex and it will therefore be important to discuss with them how that relationship might continue, especially if you have children. It will help you if your family members resist the urge to become overly hostile towards your ex. Their anger will only worsen your relationship with your ex and may make you bitter, so be wary when your family's communication with your ex becomes strained. You may need to put an emotional boundary in place if your family's response to the relationship breakdown is unhelpful, and it may mean limiting what you say to them about it.

It is natural to seek help from your parents at such a time, but you should guard against becoming overly dependent on them once the immediate crisis has passed.

In-laws

If you don't have children, it may well be appropriate just to let the relationships with your ex's family fizzle out. If you do have children, however, your in-laws are your children's relatives and, unless the relationship is dangerously destructive, it should be maintained so that your children can continue to know and see their grandparents.

> One woman said, "I never spoke to my in-laws about my ex (their son) – I only talked about our children. You have to choose to keep strife out of your relationship with your in-laws, and not talking to them about my ex really helped. After seven years of hard battling, my mother-in-law now rings me and invites my children to see her on a more regular basis."

It may seem hard at the beginning, but if you have children, aim to keep the door of friendship open to your in-laws. Once the initial stress of breakdown is behind you, your children will reap the rewards of a good relationship with all their grandparents, which can be very important for them.

Personal exercise

How has your separation or divorce affected your relationships, and how are you managing them?

Katie

My divorce had far wider consequences for my relationships than I would initially have imagined. It was far more than just one relationship ending. All my relationships were affected – some for the better and, sadly, some for the worse. It is immensely difficult to manage all the shifting sands. In a matter of weeks, everything had changed dramatically.

I had been with my husband for about fourteen years; we had effectively grown up together. His parents seemed like a second set of parents to me and it was several months before I realized, with much sadness, that I would more or less have to stop seeing them – it was just too much of a painful reminder of what I had lost. I still love them deeply but, for now at least, our contact will have to be limited to an annual Christmas card.

After fourteen years, the vast majority of our friends were joint friends. I knew that, although it was my husband's choice to leave, it would be tough for him too, and he would need some support. Although I found it immensely difficult to do, I backed away from those friends I felt he was perhaps closest too. This wasn't solely motivated by the fact that I still cared for him and wanted him to have the support he needed; it also involved a degree of self-preservation. It was painful to hear about what he was doing, thinking, or feeling, so it was better for me not to be spending time with his confidants. It is a horrible, horrible time – separating possessions at the end of a relationship tears at your heart, but dividing friends feels infinitely worse.

What was the reaction from friends?

I was incredibly fortunate in my friends, as they were brilliantly supportive, but there were a few odd and surprising reactions. In some places where I had previously been welcomed I was viewed with mistrust. It was as if they imagined that my husband's infidelity had somehow rubbed off on me and turned me into some kind of predatory husband-stealer. Equally baffling were the propositions from married male friends – how on earth could they imagine I would be interested in an affair when I had just learned firsthand how painful it is to be cheated on?! It is true what they say, that tough times really sort the wheat from the chaff. True friends step up in wonderful ways to support you, and the rest will fall away.

Divorce and separation, like anything emotional, can be a bit socially awkward. Friends who want to help just don't know how. They know they can't wave a magic wand and it is uncomfortable seeing someone you care about in distress. Sometimes this awkwardness causes friends to withdraw, which can heap even more pain on an already deeply hurtful situation. Happily, on the advice of a friend I found an easy way to deal with this. It was as simple as asking for the type of support I wanted.

Everyone has different skills and character strengths. Thinking about what I needed, matching that to a particular friend and then just asking, made it easier for my friends and family to help me. It was a real win–win case; I got the support I needed and they told me they felt relieved that they could actually do something to help. So I went out dancing with the chatty, sociable types, opened my heart to the good listeners, and asked the practical ones for help with legal matters.

What were the difficult moments?

Good friends love you warts and all – and our friends are that type, so it was natural that, although they were shocked, angry, and saddened by my husband's affair, they didn't – to their credit – turn their back on him. I love them for that but I wouldn't be very honest if I didn't admit that it was painful and felt like another betrayal at times. In my head I know that that wasn't what they intended, but sometimes my feelings lagged behind the thought. For them it must have been a difficult balancing act.

Two years on and it is sadly still an issue. My friends are currently organizing a group get-together. For the first time since the divorce they have invited my ex-husband and his partner (the lady he had the affair with) as well as me. It is so difficult to know the right thing to do. If I go, then perhaps it will be an opportunity to put the past to rest. I can't imagine we will ever have a close friendship again, but it would be amazing if we could just be comfortable in each other's presence so that we can all enjoy being a happy group of old friends again. I haven't seen my ex for over a year and have never met his partner. I don't know how I will react – although I am fairly certain it won't be a walk in the park. I don't want to cause a scene or make anyone uncomfortable.

Did your social life change?

I think one of the hardest things for me was that, despite having wonderful friends, I felt that overnight I just didn't fit in with them any more. I was thirty when my husband walked out and all my friends were couples and most were either new or expectant parents. Being suddenly single in my thirties meant that the whole rhythm of my life changed, while my friends' lives were heading in a totally different direction. I wanted to be going out in the evenings, meeting new people. They were up to their elbows in nappies and desperate for a good night's sleep.

Living alone, I suddenly had aeons of time on my own and just didn't know what to do with myself. It was tough to start with, but it actually turned out to have a good side. For the first time in my life I was able to please myself about what I wanted to do. I took up a musical instrument, joined art and dance classes, and started to develop new social circles. It became an exercise in learning who I was and what I wanted.

There was a time when I would cheerfully have punched the next person who told me I should "embrace the freedom" of being single – but actually they were right. Once you get to the point of accepting your new situation and trying to make the best of it, you discover that there is a world of fun and exciting times out there.

TOOLBOX TO TAKE AWAY
Dealing with other relationships

Managing friendships:

Recognize that friendships are affected: some friendships change; new ones start

Don't take it personally when things change

Seek out a trusted friend to support you and to challenge you

Mutual friends are difficult to manage; don't use them to gain information about your ex

Social life:

You can't change your friends' actions – you can change your reaction

Big events can be awkward – have a standard response to questions on your relationship

Just say yes, just say no

Start something new – something that you want to do

Parents and siblings:

Our family relationships also change

Resist encouraging family members to be hostile to the ex

In-laws:

Without children, it is best not to continue communication with in-laws

With children, in-laws are your kids' relations and this needs to go on

Coping at work:

Protect your work environment: keep it as a sanctuary

Tell someone at work – your boss/a colleague

Try to minimize change at work during the period of upheaval

Chapter 8

Children

"When I think about my parents' split, it makes me feel alone, unwanted, and upset. I am the only one of my friends this has happened to. They always look happy. I try to hide it when I feel sad."

Child with divorcing parents

"I remember once on my birthday I was playing in a school match and my parents both came to watch me. They didn't have to talk to each other – just to be there for my birthday. It was so good to see them together – it was one of the best days of my life."

Child with divorcing parents

Please note: Many parents feel inadequate when they think in depth about how well they manage or relate to their children. Being a separated or divorced parent is an additional huge challenge and amplifies those negative feelings immensely. This chapter sets out practical advice to help you parent your children better. If you find yourself full of guilt, stop, pause, do something different that you enjoy, and return later to draw out the positive points from this chapter.

If you have children, your separation will impact directly on your relationship with them and the way you parent together.

This can be enormously challenging. It is often hard enough to get yourself through the breakdown and divorce, let alone trying to be a great parent at the same time.

I will outline some practical advice that will help both you and your ex to parent in a better way, but, whatever your situation, this is an arduous journey. It is helpful to look at these issues from three perspectives:

1. The children's perspective

2. The perspective of the parent who is *not* regularly with their children

3. The perspective of the parent who is *more regularly* with their children.

From the outset, we need to be honest about the challenges of being a parent when you are dealing with the biggest crisis in your life. Some parents may jump straight to this section in the book with the sole focus of helping their children more. That sentiment is very honourable, but it needs to be balanced with the fact that the best thing for your children is for you, as a parent, to be healed and restored. If the parents are working well together then the children will be less affected by the relationship breakdown.

That said, this crisis will have an impact on your children, and you have to accept this fact. Statistics on the impact in general show that children of separated parents have a higher chance of: suffering academically; having health problems; being more aggressive; and taking these scars into their future relationships. However, there *is* good news – these statistics do not mean that *your* child will be affected.

I have seen many, many children thrive in separated families because of the amazing work done by individual parents or by both parents together. These children have had to face enormous difficulties in their lives but have come out of it as mature, healthy, and responsible adults.

Age-specific issues

There is no "better age" for children to experience divorce. In fact, I have seen many twenty- to thirty-year-olds profoundly affected by their parent's divorce as they try to recalibrate their life in the light of the new situation. However, children do react differently to their parents' break-up according to their age.

Birth to four years old

At this early stage it is important to allow time for both parents to bond with their baby/toddler and for the child to bond with their parents. Babies and young children understand little of what is going on but, because they are physically and emotionally dependent on their parents, they will feel vulnerable to any significant change, particularly any substantial reduction in the time spent with one parent.

Physical and emotional support from both parents for the child is important at this time.

Five to eleven years old

As awareness and understanding develop in children, they are more likely to pick up on some of the facts of your situation, and fears or fantasies may follow close behind. If one parent has left, they will fear being rejected and abandoned by the other one. They will worry that the separation was their fault and they may have many dreams and ideas about their parents getting back together.

Simple, clear communication with children, especially when they raise the subject, can be important in countering unreasonable thoughts. Make sure to listen to what they say, however crazy it may be.

Twelve to eighteen years old

This period of life marks significant physical and emotional changes for children, who long to feel "normal". They are starting to work out more about their own personality and to think more about relationships in general. Overlay this with a crisis between their parents, and you have an explosive mix of feelings, which they have to learn to deal with.

These children will, much like adults, express their emotions in different ways. Some will retreat into silence (possibly covering anger or fear), some will blame parents regularly and become bitter, and others may express their anger in various ways.

This age group will automatically have to take on more responsibility if they live in a single-parent home or if either of their parents is struggling to cope with the relationship breakdown.

Encourage them to understand their thoughts and feelings and allow them to express themselves in a healthy way. Listening to them (without giving advice) will make them feel valued and enable them to work out what their feelings are.

These are the main considerations for particular ages; however, the issues raised for one age group can still be relevant to the other groups. For example, bonding is essential in the early years but is also important for a seven-year-old boy and a fourteen-year-old girl. Similarly, ensuring that a child does not feel responsible is vital when they are young, but also when they get older.

Telling the children

The first time that you tell the children is a momentous point in everyone's life, and should be done with great care. This is what one mother wrote about her experiences:

Even nearly five years on, I find it horribly painful to recall the day we told our children – a daughter and son then aged twelve and eight respectively – that their father was leaving.

We set a date and time for telling them – after lunch on a Sunday so there would be plenty of time to console them – and, tacitly acknowledging it would probably be a day that would haunt us all, we rehearsed what we would say. In my case at least, the practice run also helped to minimize the chances of breaking down in front of the children. I felt an overwhelming maternal protective instinct and knew we had to do it in a way that would show it was a carefully considered, mutual decision made with them in mind. Because of their ages I also knew they would need more than an evasive "Mum and Dad aren't getting on very well at the moment" if they were to understand why their father was leaving them and their mother appeared so bereft.

"If you tell them the truth, they'll think he doesn't love them," my mother-in-law wrote in a letter I opened the day before we told them. But my husband and I both reasoned – and our counsellor concurred – that the opposite was true: that the children might feel less loved, and even some illogical sense of responsibility, if they weren't given a clear reason for the split.

Taking the children into the sitting-room for that "chat" was possibly the hardest thing I have ever done. This, I felt, would be a watershed in their lives, a brutal shattering of childhood innocence – and I had failed to prevent it. My husband had volunteered to break the news, and his words are seared into my memory: "You may have noticed that I have been rather distracted recently and that Mum has been unhappy. Well, there's a reason: I've developed strong feelings for someone else and that has hurt Mum very badly. We feel that, for now, it's best for everyone if I move out."

I will always remember the look of stunned incomprehension on the children's faces. Our son said he had no idea anything was wrong as he had never heard us arguing like some of his friends' parents. Our daughter said she had occasionally heard raised voices when she was in bed, but had accepted our explanation that we were just tired.

We reassured them that we loved them absolutely and that they were not to blame in any way; that they wouldn't have to leave their home and would see their father regularly; that it was a grown-up problem and they could trust us to do what was best for everyone. I was glad I had insisted on rehearsing answers to the questions they were bound to ask. Naturally they wanted to know who the woman was, but we said that at this point we felt her identity wasn't relevant, as she didn't live anywhere near us. Perhaps one day in the future when things weren't so raw, we said, if they were still curious we would tell them.

Our aim then, as now, was to give them enough detail but not too much; to make them feel as secure and loved as possible without burdening them with our problems. To maintain a sense of unity we then all squished on the sofa and watched a film. Later, in keeping with their respective personalities, our son wept openly while our daughter silently withdrew to process the unwanted information.

The next morning I forewarned the children's teachers that they might need extra support. It was a torturous time; but my now ex-husband and I have worked so hard at staying civil and not criticizing each other in front of the children that, years later, I think we can feel quite proud of how we have dealt with the situation. We're not textbook-perfect, but we are in regular communication about the children. It has benefited us all that we have continued to do some things as a family, such as school events, birthday dinners, and early Christmases, and never asked them to take sides.

Recently my children and I were discussing the day of the announcement. I felt a huge wave of relief when my now thirteen-year-old son said casually that he didn't think about it any more. The fact that the event isn't filed away in the "Worst Day of My Life" compartment of his memory seems like an affirmation that, however much his father and I got wrong, we got something as right as we could.

1. The children's perspective

The following quotes represent a number of the thoughts and feelings of children aged between eleven and eighteen, who come from a broad range of backgrounds and situations:

When I think about my parents' split, it makes me feel alone, unwanted, and upset. I am the only one of my friends this has happened to. They always look happy. I try to hide it when I feel sad.

I have found it difficult to concentrate on my work.

I don't feel we have a normal family without a dad. My mates say it's OK and that they understand how I feel, but they don't.

I hate to be singled out. I just want to be like any other kid and feel normal.

The worst thing is being confused, not really knowing what's going on. I wish they would be straight with me. They try to protect me but it only makes things worse.

I can now get angry quite easily. Really angry. Takes me a while to simmer down.

I feel the pressure of being the man in the house, now Dad's gone.

I can't relate to my parents and won't talk to them. I just don't trust them any more.

The worst thing is not being able to please them both — for example if one didn't want me to see the other.

I'm more bothered about how Mum is than about how I am. I feel a lot of sympathy with her as she's been left and is just expected to cope.

I don't want my dad to spoil me or try to be a buddy or mate. I want him to be my dad, somebody I can rely on. Just Dad.

I don't have any brothers or sisters so I haven't got anyone to talk to about the divorce. I wish I did.

I can't really talk about the divorce to my parents. It's like talking to them about their wrongdoing and I find that really hard.

Mum did some terrible things. But she's still my Mum, and I love her.

I hate being lied to. However bad the truth is, it is always going to be better than lies.

When Mum's upset, I sort of have to look after her. Makes me feel like the parent.

When my parents are angry and crying, I somehow think I'm part of their break-up and feel responsible. I feel I have to make them happy, which puts a lot on me, I think.

Because I was living with Mum, I took her side, but in fact that wasn't fair on my dad. I now know it takes two people to break up a marriage, not just one person. I don't want to have to choose.

I miss being normal. I don't like my dad saying, "How are you?" and being all heavy. I just want to have a normal chat.

I hate it when one parent digs for information out of me on the other parent. I am not going to be a go-between. It's not their business what goes on.

I don't always want to have to see Dad with his new girlfriend. I want to see him alone, just me and him.

Sometimes my parents say things I just don't want to hear. I worry that if I talk to my mum, she'll say something that I don't want to hear, and then I'll wish I hadn't spoken to her.

I remember once on my birthday I was playing in a school match and my parents both came to watch me. They didn't have to talk to each other – just to be there for my birthday. It was so good to see them together – it was one of the best days of my life.

These children were asked what they found helpful in coping with these feelings. This is what they said:

Talk to someone neutral.

Talk to a pet.

Write a diary.

Think of your situation as normal.

Be free to cry. Some people think boys don't cry but I have cried a lot, and it's been really helpful.

Talk to a camera – you can say anything you don't have the nerve to say to your parents directly.

Tell your parents you do not want to hear them bad-mouth each other.

Decide to make your own decisions about who's right and who's wrong, and not to listen to just one parent.

Really try to think of yourself as normal. Have normal chats. Be normal.

There is a lot to take in here, but some clear principles can be seen:

1. Children want to be normal – at school, with their peers, with their parents, with others. They do not want to be thrust into a world of "heavy" stuff. They want to go on as usual;

2. They want to be kept right out of the conflict between their parents; and

3. They want to find ways to express what they are feeling – their suggestions are talk to a friend/pet/someone neutral/write a diary/cry. These are all ways for them to manage their thoughts and feelings.

Annie talked about her situation in Chapter 2, and here she discusses things that have been helpful for her:

First, I have tried to find ways for the children to be able to express their feelings. This is much harder in practice than it may seem, because they will be guarded in what they say to either parent for fear of letting the other one down. A safe and neutral place must be found for them.

What happened with us is that there were a number of problems early on in the separation and the children were finding it tough. I asked one of my children's godparents, who is a trained therapist, to set up a meeting around our kitchen table with us all there, so that my ex and I could listen to the children. The deal was that we would not interrupt, defend, or justify ourselves. We were just there to listen. It was scary – what were they going to say? But in fact it was really helpful. I needed to hear how much they minded me crying and getting upset. What happened was that the children opened their hearts and let it all out. They said what they really felt and it was incredibly helpful to us all.

Try to set up a safe place where they can talk, with or without you there. If you can encourage or nurture any relationships that your children may have with other adults who would be wise listeners, then do so. Do whatever you can to provide your children with the opportunity to express how they are feeling to somebody neutral – maybe even a professional therapist or mediator. It will be such a help to them.

Second, we can help our children by recognizing any signs of anger. Sometimes we are not even aware that we are angry and yet it affects every aspect of our behaviour and makes it hard to move on in peace.

The first step is to recognize the anger; the next is to work out what it is that is making us angry; and the final step is to let it out constructively. It is fine to feel angry – in fact, we will all experience anger at times in our lives. It is what we do with it that matters.

For me, that meant throwing cushions at the sofa while letting rip about what I was angry about. My children have at times found it incredibly helpful to throw cushions and let it all out, and I give them permission to say anything they want as they throw them against a wall.

The third thing that helped our children was forgiveness. When we forgive, we find freedom and the ability to move forward in peace, and our children can do this too. For parents there are two aspects to our forgiveness: we need to forgive our ex for the hurt we feel as a *partner; and in addition we need to forgive our ex (and ourselves) for the hurt, often deeper, that we feel in seeing our children suffer. For many, that is harder than forgiving our ex for what has happened between us. Remember that we cannot forgive on behalf of our children; only they can do that. But we can forgive our ex for the pain we feel as a parent when we see them suffer.*

Our children will most likely need to forgive both parents and sometimes other people as well. The only way to help them do this is to lead by example. An amazing example of this is Gee Walker, the mother of Anthony, a teenage boy who was brutally murdered in 2005 for no reason other than the colour of his skin. Gee has given a number of interviews and speaks of her intense pain: of lying awake crying for him and her loss. She also speaks of forgiveness, saying, "I cannot hate; hate is what killed Anthony. I have to forgive them."

When it comes to her children, this is what she said: "I have always taught my children to forgive; it's part of our way of life. So when Anthony was killed, I had to lead by example. My desire was to portray love. I can't expect people to forgive, love, and not to hate, if I hate and do not show forgiveness. I have to lead by example and hopefully, when my children see me, it will help them too."

Another aspect of this is that I try to speak about their father with praise and point out all the good things that we have, thanks to his provision. I try to show the ways in which he has been good to us. If forgiveness flows from us, it will help them, and in their own time they may come to forgive us both for what they have been through.

Regardless of the role we may have played in the breakdown of our marriage, our children never asked for this to happen. Their whole lives were turned upside down. We are all trying to heal in our own way and I know that the healthier I am emotionally, the better it is for the children. I know that can seem like a huge pressure, especially in the early days when you can hardly get out of bed. So get as much help as possible for yourself from friends, family, church, self-help groups, counselling, and therapy (for instance anger workshops!). You can pass what you learn on to your children at a time and in a way that is appropriate for them.

Personal exercise

What are the issues that your children find hardest at the moment?

2. The perspective of the parent who is *not* regularly with their children

Our children have a right to have a relationship with both their parents. One of the hardest aspects of separation is releasing them to be with the other parent and therefore being separated from them. It may be that you are separated from your children for short periods while they are with their other parent, or it may be that you are separated for long periods and see them very little. Both situations are hard.

This is what one dad living away from his children wrote:

The break-up of our marriage and the end of all the aspirations I had had for our future life together were like a bereavement. So was the realization that I was never going to live in the same house as my children again. I had to give myself time, space, and permission to cry. I wept from my gut for about twenty minutes every day for six months. Thereafter it eased, but it continued for about eighteen months in total. I found that letting out the pain made me feel better, and I am sure it helped the healing process.

My wife and her partner began living together shortly after we had separated. The thought of it filled my mind all the time. Above all, the idea of my son with "the other man" caused real pain. I was afraid of losing him and of being replaced as a father. The mere thought that our child was forced to live in this situation drove me crazy. I had these thoughts continuously in my mind, which made me feel bad, but I couldn't escape them.

If there is a real "desert experience", if there is a "dark night of the soul", then I have endured those moments. Moments of darkness and solitude when nothing can give you relief. Moments when no one can comprehend your situation and you feel misunderstood by everyone; when pain leaves you breathless. Feeling rejected, "thrown away"; finding yourself without an identity, profoundly destabilized, and estranged from the world. I could not watch our son without feeling a lump in my throat.

It hurts to be separated from your children. It is important to acknowledge that and to grieve for the loss of a close everyday relationship.

It is hard enough not living with your children any more, but if the resident parent is also seeking to obstruct your time with them, it can be deeply painful. Here are some suggestions on how to manage the situation, but as I offer them I must emphasize that in no way am I suggesting that they will minimize the pain of being cut off:

- Make sure that you have an outlet for your feelings, such as writing them in a journal or speaking to someone else who is going through the same thing. Beware of the feelings building up or becoming overwhelming.

- Do all you can to set up contact arrangements that are best for the children. Many parents handle this with sensitivity, wisdom, and a focus on what works well for the children, which may include being flexible with arrangements when new situations arise. It may be necessary to use neutral outsiders or mediators to help with any difficult conversations that are required to achieve this.

- Even if you are not seeing your children regularly, it is important to stay in touch. You may like to write them a weekly letter, or send an email or regular texts. If it does not cause stress, then a regular chat on the phone can be a good idea, ensuring that the privacy of the other parent is respected and that they do not feel bombarded by you. Skype calls are cost-effective and add a very real dimension to the conversation because of their video facility.

- In these emails/letters/phone calls, make sure you remember the important events in your child's life – term dates, exams, trips away, special days at school, etc. Show them that you are involved in their life, even if you are not there.

- As far as you can, encourage your ex to help the children communicate with you. Children normally follow their parent's lead, and it is therefore the responsibility of parents to support this regular contact with the absent parent and help the children to be proactive. For instance, Christmas and birthday cards for the non-resident parent are important for both children and parent, but this may require the support of the resident parent.

- If you end up in litigation, always be aware of what is best for the children. Avoid slipping into situations that will result in you and your ex using your children as pawns in the middle of your battle. Keep asking yourself the question "What is the best solution here for the children?"

- Be reassured that, however much pain and stress the other parent is causing you, your children are created 50 per cent from Mum and 50 per cent from Dad. They will still love her as their mum or him as their dad. One of the best ways of loving your children is to respect your ex as a parent. This is hugely difficult following a relationship breakdown, particularly if he or she is the person who is causing you so much pain. However, you must always strive to speak kindly and respectfully of the other parent. Even if you do not feel very loving, guard what you say and how you behave. Children need the emotional freedom to be able to love both their parents.

• Be patient and persistent. You will always be your children's father or mother. As children get older they can make more decisions by themselves, and if you have kept in touch there may come a time when you have more contact and a deeper relationship.

Bill talks about his experience of being a father but not living in the same house as his children:

Penny and I had our ups and downs, but we had what I thought was a good relationship.

Things started to get difficult when Penny had an affair with one of my good friends, whom I'd known since I was eight. It was really tough to deal with but we had two kids and I didn't want to leave.

When I received a new job offer based in the USA, we decided it would be good for us all to go. We got through this difficult period because I think Penny had been able to close the door on the problems, but I certainly hadn't. We had flown 5,000 miles away from the affair but it was unresolved for me and I was in a pretty bad way: very angry, very bitter, very confused, and fundamentally betrayed.

We had two more kids in the USA but soon our marriage was in a bad way again. My work didn't help as it involved very long hours. I left home with everybody asleep and when I got home I was shattered and exhausted; it was a very punishing schedule.

Then Penny met Rob, and it soon became very obvious that there was something going on. You recognize the warning signs even if you aren't looking for them. It was history repeating itself. All those horrible emotions that I had tried to deal with previously surged up again and it was ghastly. It was truly awful. It's very hard to describe in words. To make me suffer like this again was beyond cruel, and she made no attempt to hide the affair.

I moved just down the road to allow a bit of space between us, but it was all very confusing for the children. Penny set up a strict regime of controlled contact with the kids even though I was close by and we were just having some time apart. I wanted to try to present a normal front to the children but, on more than one occasion, I had the door slammed in my face with the children in the sitting room watching. It was hard for me and it was certainly hard for them.

By that stage I was a wreck. I was working at air traffic control, which suspended me from my duties, saying, "We can't have you in working in your state of mind; you're going to end up making a mistake and someone's going to get killed." It was the sensible thing to do, but very demoralizing.

We agreed on a trial separation, just to see if that would help in some way, but I'm not too sure what we were hoping to achieve in six months. I gave up my job and moved back to the UK, still with the hope of trying to fix things.

We got divorced, but sadly that is just the beginning of the legal story. After five years of vast expense we continue to try to resolve both the finances and my contact with the children.

As regards contact, the only time that I can see the children is when they and I are on holiday. So far that's been about twice a year and it's worked, but it's been open to last minute changes and lots of frustrations.

In the early stages I didn't phone the children enough and Penny didn't encourage them to contact me. Now I send them letters and postcards and I try to phone them regularly.

I have now successfully managed to persuade my eldest son to create a Skype account on the computer for himself. I've been pushing for this for six years because it's free and phone calls are so expensive. Even so, any telephone or Skype contact is still difficult. I'll phone and won't get any answer, or perhaps their mobile is not charged, or maybe Penny doesn't answer because she knows it's me calling.

The fact is that I don't get Christmas cards, I don't get birthday cards, I don't get letters, Easter cards, postcards, or anything. So I'm really having to push it and that's tough, because you end up being cast as a bit of a bully and that's not the role I'm trying to play here – I'm just trying to be a father.

It's the worst thing I've had to cope with, being a parent who does not see his children very often. The hardest thing is missing the sheer joy, the tactile joy, of being able to hold them. My youngest son is still young enough and light enough to be picked up, and you can't put a price on that. Skype calls are good but being able to hold your children, touch them, give them an embrace, a hug, and a kiss is truly priceless and not being able to do that, even on a remotely regular basis, is very hard. It is agony, and over the last year I've not seen them at all, which is definitely a low point.

You've got to be really pragmatic with yourself and say, "This is the situation; I've got to deal with it and not dwell on it." That is sometimes easier said than done, but I would encourage you to find a different and regular focus for your energies. It's amazing how focusing your mind in a different direction for a while can liberate you from those bad feelings.

Forgiveness has helped me to develop a healthy, almost casual, indifference to the past and the person who generated all that pain. It's an ongoing process, but I can say after six years that it's nice to be there. You can wake up and the past doesn't bother you. When you reach that point you know you're in a better place.

Having that first Skype call with the kids and seeing them on the screen was a mountain-top experience for me a month ago. They were animated, they were bubbling, and they were joyful. I was almost in tears and I thought, "Wow, this is it; after six years I can finally speak to the kids via the TV screen."

My parents got divorced when I was very young and both my mum and my dad subsequently remarried. What my brother and I loved was my father being able to get on really well with my stepfather because there wasn't any bad history. We all got on well. I had two key male role models in my life and enjoyed really good relationships because there wasn't any messiness. I really look forward to a time when I can engage with Penny and her new husband on a much healthier level.

Over the last six years I've moved house fourteen times, seen the death of my grandmother, to whom I was extremely close, been close to suicide, not seen my kids much, and am still going through a difficult legal battle. Holding it together has been tough at times, but it's been the making of me.

Personal exercise

How can you best keep in contact with your children?

3. The perspective of the parent who is *more regularly* with their children

Annie describes her experience and the lessons she learned about caring for her children during her separation and subsequent divorce:

Our children were eleven, nine, and seven when we split up and I was their full-time carer. If I look back over the early years I can honestly say that I have done most of the things on the list entitled "Never do this to your children", including screaming at their father in front of them, banging my head against the wall, slamming down the phone and calling him rude names, bad-mouthing him when they can hear, and crying constantly for about two years.

I have learned that these actions damage my children and me much more than they hurt the person they were intended to hurt, and over the last few years I have tried to change some of this behaviour! The initial weeks and months of intense feelings of anger, betrayal, jealousy, deep hurt, and full-on hatred were often indescribable to the outside world, although you may well understand their severity. I became very isolated and spent most of the time crying in the garden with a glass of wine and a cigarette (although I had not smoked for fourteen years).

The isolation was compounded by the fact that the one person I wanted to talk to was the one person who had in a single day become the one person I could no longer confide in – the person I had discussed every joy and sadness with was no longer available to me, and that was truly devastating. I had heard all the stuff about how to help children through separation and divorce, but the reality is that I was just trying to survive, and doing any more than that was impossible.

Letting the children go to the other parent

For me, one of the most agonizing, and therefore volatile, times was when the children were collected to go away with their father. These points really fed my isolation and feelings of abandonment. So I learned to arrange either for a friend to be with me in the kitchen or to have somewhere to go straight afterwards.

This helped the children to leave knowing that I was OK (on previous occasions I would be crying, which was very difficult for them) and they were free to enjoy their time with Daddy. It also meant that I could cry and talk with my friend until I felt that I could cope again.

I think that your children going away from you is the most painful thing in the world, but it does get better! I still sometimes call someone who I know will understand. I simply tell them the children have just gone and I want to talk to someone! I also try to put something nice in the diary for myself when the children go away for the weekend, such as seeing friends or going to the movies, or sometimes I choose to do nothing at all (but only as an active choice).

I remember a girlfriend of mine, who went through this years before I did, saying that I would begin to love the times when the children went off with their father. I thought, "What does she know? I will never feel like that!" But I do now – I love the peace of having the house to myself, as it is a rare pleasure when you usually have three teenagers hanging around with their assorted friends.

I have found that it is really helpful for the children if I release them with my blessing to their father so that they can enjoy their time with him. This means saying to them before they go, "I hope you have a really good time with Daddy this weekend. I am going to be doing X and Y, but do call me if you would like to." This allows them to have fun with Daddy, because I am going to be fine. I found that calling them while they were away was quite hard for them and painful for me. The important thing is that they know I am available if needed, but they don't have to call me.

Meeting the ex

My ex and I used to have a termly meeting to discuss dates, times, school matters, etc. In the early days these were low-level battlegrounds. I longed to see him, mainly wanting him to look awful so that I would feel better, and eager to hear about his life so that I could wallow in self-pity afterwards. All this was going on in my head while we were talking about the children's logistics. No wonder I was going mad! One of the ways round these totally insane times was to have an agenda for what needed to be discussed. I would print out my diary with what suited me and the children and then we would discuss it and come to a compromise on times and dates. This gave me a structure for the meeting rather than a chaotic mishmash of feelings.

Having a trustworthy friend with no outside agenda is so helpful. And don't choose someone who dislikes your ex! But do choose someone who loves you and wants the best for you and your children, yet is willing to challenge you. It is very important that it should be someone you will listen to if they say you are out of order.

By processing the emotions with a trustworthy friend elsewhere, I found it easier to handle problems with my ex, as our meetings were more businesslike. For example, if something I wasn't expecting came up in the meeting, I was able to say, "I will think about that and get back to you" or "I don't feel ready to comment on that at the moment; I will email you later." All these responses give you time to think and to call your trustworthy friend to talk it through. It is very empowering to realize that you don't have to answer straight away.

These are new ways of behaving and can feel strange, because this person was supposed to be your soulmate. You would never have said to your husband or wife, "I will think about it and get back to you later." But things have changed and our way of relating to each other must also change. When we try these new ways and it goes well it is very encouraging, and we can try again next time. For me it was about becoming an adult in my relationship with my ex. I think that the process of relationship breakdown can often push us back into childlike responses and I needed to grow up and take responsibility for where we had got to, but it wasn't easy!

Information about your ex

When the children first started going to their father I wanted to know everything: "What did they do?" "How was Daddy?" "Did Daddy cook?" In the past he had only made tomato soup (and then only if I was ill), so I longed to know how they had survived the weekend! It was a nightmare for the children, as whatever they said was wrong. If their dad did cook, I'd say: "Well he hadn't helped me for fifteen years." And if they ate in a restaurant, I'd come back with: "Well it's OK for some!" It put the children in an impossible position because, however awful he appeared to me, he was their father and they loved him warts and all.

When we criticize our ex, we are also criticizing our children, as half of them comes from the other parent. I find it useful to visualize this when I feel like saying something unhelpful. Interestingly, now that I have got to the advanced stage of actually defending my ex to my children. My daughter, who is now sixteen, recently said to me, "When I am annoyed with Dad, please don't defend him! I am allowed to be angry with him sometimes and I don't want you telling me he is doing his best — just listen, please."

I have learned just how awful these times of crossover between families can be. To move between two very different households with different rules and guidelines is difficult for adults, never mind children. For our children it is particularly difficult, especially as we are the two people who used to live together with the same rules and guidelines.

What I have found easiest for us all is not to ask any questions about their time with their father apart from the very vague "Did you have a lovely time with Daddy?" or "Was it fun seeing Daddy's new dog?" Then when the dust has settled a bit we go for a walk. This has lots of advantages: when walking side by side you are close and can hold hands and have intimacy without eye contact. Also, there are lots of distractions if things get tough.

I find that this way they will talk about the bits they need or want me to hear. If you find something hard to discuss with your kids, it might be good to say, "Perhaps we can talk about that later when I can think more clearly" and then remember to come back to it! Sometimes I will say, "Do you want me just to listen or do you want my opinion or advice?" As they get older, this can really help *both them and you. If something special crops up, I might write a note to discuss it with their father or send an email. If you were still together a lot of these issues would be a natural part of everyday conversation, so I try to maintain that sense of immediacy.*

Coping with your ex at school

For about two years, I was unable to manage any contact with the children's father at their schools. I could not sit with him or talk to him. Slowly, through trial and error, we learned to manage to be parents together at the schools. We even drive to school in the same car, sometimes even with me in the front seat. To start with I would put a child in the front, as sitting next to my ex in a car was too intimate for me and I was scared that we would slip back into old roles that were now inappropriate. It was a helpful boundary for me. Each time we do something together at school, I see how much it means to the children. It enables them to be the same as other children with two parents who appear to be relatively normal.

Dealing with feelings

No matter how much you try to hold it together, you will get it wrong, especially when your child tells you something upsetting or shocking about the ex. For example, when my kids said to me, "Did you know Daddy is going to Morocco with his girlfriend?", I really went haywire. I immediately rang their father and screamed and shouted at him to come back and discuss the matter with me now. I also told him what I thought of him in small, bite-sized words – all of this with the children standing in the hall looking terrified – not my finest moment as a mother! Now my prayer is to try not to overreact. Then I try to get to a phone as quickly as possible to call anyone I know who is in, who can listen, and who will be understanding.

At these times it is so important to have someone who can ask the right questions. For example, "What was the most important thing about this for you?"; "What did it trigger in you?

Loneliness? Abandonment? Hurt? Anger?"; "What does it mean to the children?"; "What do you want to do about it?"; "What can you do?"; "Is it actually anything to do with you?" That last one is very tough, because I often found that in fact the thing had nothing to do with me, except that it highlighted my inability to let go of my husband! So my advice would be: get on the phone and offload to someone who will not be damaged by what you say; process what has happened to you; and then make a positive plan.

Pinpointing emotional triggers

Another thing that I am learning is to recognize the triggers that pull me down. I have found it really helpful to work out what my personal triggers are and I have found them to be common in many other people. For me it is abandonment, rejection, and when I feel life really closing in again. Some days I will still cry at the loss – the loss of family, the loss of the dream of my marriage, the loss of the future together with our grandchildren. I try to look at reality – "What is really happening here?" and then attempt to separate the feelings from the facts. Sometimes I am so full of fear, and then I have to stop and look hard at the reality of the situation. Often if I can do that, I can unravel the fear and face the reality.

New situations

My ex got remarried a few years ago and, although I was happy for him and for the children, I knew that this would be a particularly difficult time for me. So I went on holiday with a girlfriend and came back refreshed, tanned, and having read six books... bliss! It is not always possible to anticipate difficult times, but that was one I knew was coming, so I looked after myself. What I had totally failed to anticipate was the children coming home with the wedding photographs, which they really wanted me to see – that was very painful for me.

I have broken most of the rules in the book, and yet I believe that, with the help of a number of practical steps, my ex and I are moving into a better phase of successful co-parenting, and this has to be the very best thing for our children.

A goal for parents

The intention is that we should shift from being parents who are married, to separate parents who successfully manage their children together.

One helpful process in implementing this shift is to write a letter to the other parent, setting out guidelines for how you intend to parent together successfully. A draft letter is shown below (and is also on our website, www.restoredlives.org). This letter helps you to focus on what is important now, and also acts as a great summary and action plan for you in the future.

You may want to tailor this letter to your own circumstances, for example by including any other specific goals that you have, such as plans for Christmas, holidays, birthdays, schools, etc.

Shared Parenting Letter

Dear_____,

I am writing about our children. Whatever our thoughts are about each other, our children have never asked for this to happen. My hope is that we can put aside our issues and still be good parents to them, even though we will live apart.

The question for us is how do we shift from being parents who live together, to being separate adults who share the parenting role successfully? To start this process I have put down my thoughts below, but I would welcome your comments or additional ideas so that we can agree on the way that we share our parenting roles for the benefit of the children.

1. It would be good if we could tell them together that we are separating. We can tell them that this is not their fault, that we both love them, and that they will be spending lots of time with both of us.

2. Let's commit to be respectful about each other in front of the children. I recognize that they love you and the best thing for them is for me not to make unkind comments about you to them. I will find opportunities to talk about you in a positive way with them. Let's try to stop others, like our parents or friends, from being disrespectful about either of us in front of the children.

3. When we are in conflict about something, let's deal with it privately and not in front of the children.

4. At times of handover, let's be polite and friendly to each other, as these can be stressful moments for everyone.

5. When they are with me, I will not ask the children for information about you or your life, as it's not fair for them.

6. Let's make sure that we communicate directly with each other about their arrangements and their needs so that we never use them as the communication link between us.

7. Please can we try to agree similar house rules or boundaries together? We may not always agree, but at least then we can tell them that we've spoken about it, and that we know something's allowed in one of our homes and not the other. My hope is that they will experience us parenting together in this way, and will not be able to play us off against each other.

8. Can we try to attend some school events together, and sit next to each other at parents' evenings or school plays/matches, etc? I know that the children will appreciate this enormously it if we can manage it in a polite way.

9. We will have a lot of arrangements to sort out, such as when they spend time with us both. It won't always be easy and we won't always agree, but I will commit to listen to you, and do my best to be constructive and polite in finding solutions to any disagreements. Let's agree to try to find solutions that work for both of us, rather than talking about winning and losing on every issue.

10. You share responsibility with me for our children and therefore, if any serious difficulties or challenges arise, I will discuss these issues with you rather than turn to others. Even though we have separate personal lives, I will make the effort to communicate with you about these issues straight away.

If we both follow this agreement, I believe that it will give our children a good hope for their future. I am confident that we can agree on the way forward for our parenting and will commit to putting all this into practise. I look forward to hearing your thoughts about how we can take this forward.

Personal exercise

What would help you in parenting your children? Print out the shared parenting letter and discuss it with your ex.

James (Annie's eldest child, aged twelve at the time)

What were your first memories of things not going very well between your mum and dad?

It was a downward spiral. I can't really put my finger on it. There was this atmosphere in the house that was slightly alien to us. One *example was when we went on holiday, and Mum and Dad both started smoking completely out of the blue. It was sort of "What is going on?" – I remember being really upset just by that change. I felt this change wasn't necessary and I didn't know why – I cried and Mum stopped smoking, which was good.*

Home was very strange around that time. I remember just crying for no reason. You couldn't put your finger on it – it was just a feeling, a hunch, but I still wouldn't have said to friends, "Oh, Mum and Dad are doing really badly"; it was just weird. Even then, I used school to get away from it all, as time to escape.

Then they sat us down and told us. It was very, very strange. My little sister (who was seven at the time) had no idea that Dad hadn't been living there for the previous week. It was just the biggest shock. I don't think we really understood that much. We weren't angry at the time, just shocked.

Then it was hugs, hugs, hugs, and goodbye, Dad. It was all a bit weird. We were dazed by it. I think it's very hard when you don't understand what's going on. Later on, I found things out and thought, "Oh my, why didn't I know that?" I get quite angry that I was so ignorant at that time. I was angry, but I didn't show it. My character became a bit more edgy. I would get angry at things that usually wouldn't bother me. I wasn't on great form for quite a while.

My brother got very angry. My little sister didn't understand much at the time, but she found it very hard when Mum slipped in the odd bad comment about Dad. She was very angry at Dad but wasn't sure why – mostly it was because she could see the state Mum was in and was really affected by that.

How did you deal with those emotions?

We had a counsellor, my godmother, and I found that really, really helpful. She was neutral and I would have sessions with her alone. I saw her once a term for about two and a half years and it was a really vital time, when everything was new and I was just trying to adjust.

All I did was cry in those sessions and I think that's really important. You try to be all strong, with "Let's help Mum through this", but in the end you're also sad and you have to get through it yourself.

By focusing on your feelings and letting them out, you discover what you actually feel, instead of just ignoring it. Instead of the simple "Oh I don't like this" thought going round and round in your head, you start to understand what's going on and why you feel a certain way. Then you can deal with it.

In the beginning I wasn't ready to talk but once I'd started, it just overflowed. You really need to get it out. She didn't drag it out of me but she asked the type of question that I always wanted people to ask in a safe environment, such as, "How do you feel? How are you doing?" Twelve-year-old boys don't generally ask that sort of thing. I did have a friend at school who was Mum's best friend's son, and he was clued up; he knew what was going on and he didn't really ask questions, but I could talk to him. It was good to know that he knew what was going on, and it wasn't just me. Otherwise you try to hide it.

How was communication in your family then?

It got really difficult. I didn't generally communicate much when I was at school — I kept to myself. At home, I thought that if I was all weak in front of Mum it would make her worse. I had to be strong for Mum, and it was difficult to express my feelings to her because I didn't want to make things worse. She already had enough on her plate without having to deal with me being all sad and annoyed as well, as it would multiply her anguish and make her feel even worse about it all. So I bottled it all up.

My brother, sister, and I didn't really communicate much between ourselves. It was each one's own fight, as it were. The times we had as a family talking around the table with my godmother, Mum, and Dad were amazing. The whole "no interruption" thing was great, as my little sister could really talk, even if it was stuff that my brother and I didn't agree with. Otherwise things like that never really come out.

After we discovered that Dad had a girlfriend we didn't see him for about seven weeks, as we were all so shocked. That was really awkward. He would then call every three to four days and speak to each of us, which was nice. It was low-key and made going to see Dad easier.

How are things now?

I think about forgiveness. It's really difficult, because you wonder, "If I forgive Dad, does that mean what he has done to us is all OK now? Or what we've done to him?" It feels slightly unnatural but it's definitely a stage I want to get to, as it will mean there is no longer any resentment and nothing there that can stop our relationship. As it's always at the back of my mind, I really want to be able to let it go.

Things with my mum have also definitely got a lot better; however, if she slips in the odd comment about Dad I still find it quite upsetting, even if it is a mundane thing. When I'm not studying I spend some time with Dad. I'm never going to be able to live day to day with both parents and I miss that; it's something you can't ever really replace, but even so it is nice to see him once in a while, and it doesn't have to be anything special.

Please note: Coping with a relationship breakdown can be hard enough on its own, but also having to guide children through this massive change can be incredibly difficult. Do not let yourself be overcome with guilt after reading this chapter. Reflect on the positive points that relate to your situation and talk to someone about any feelings of guilt that you may have. Maybe go back over the topics of acceptance and letting go.

TOOLBOX TO TAKE AWAY
Relationships with children

- *Find ways for the children to express their thoughts and feelings.*
- *Find a safe and neutral venue where children can speak.*
- *When children express themselves don't interrupt, defend, justify, or fix – just listen. Use reflective listening to bring out their thoughts.*
- *Ensure the children have regular contact with both parents.*
- *Nurture any relationships that your children have with other appropriate adults.*
- *Enable them to have space and time to let their emotions out in a constructive way.*
- *Help create an environment where the children can forgive both parents.*
- *Speak well of the other parent to the children – this will help you and them.*
- *Make sure the children know that it is not their fault.*
- *Get outside help if necessary: mediators, counsellors, doctors.*
- *Tell the school – they may be able to help.*

For parents:
- *Recognize that you will get it wrong as a parent – don't be too hard on yourself.*
- *Identify your personal triggers, such as isolation, abandonment, insensitive comments, etc.*
- *Review the way that you communicate with your ex – try businesslike meetings.*

- *Don't try to find out what is going on with your ex — it's most probably nothing to do with you now.*
- *Acknowledge that there will be differences in parenting styles, which you need to accept.*
- *Try to agree on similar rules for the two households.*

PART FIVE

AGREEING THE BIG ISSUES BETWEEN YOU

Chapter 9

Sorting out legal matters

"Communication issues were really important for me because we went through a very difficult financial divorce. We ended up in court for a whole day on the financial settlement, and it was such a bad experience – I wouldn't wish it on anyone. I came out of it in shock. I was still in shock that night in bed and my body felt as if it was in a different world."

William

"Try NOT to litigate. A divorce case will cost you time, money, and a great emotional strain even if you think you are 'in the right'. Try to settle even if the settlement is not generous to you (and mine wasn't!). At least you are free. Does it really matter if she has your lawnmower when you are living in a flat? Or your mother's piano when you can't play a note?

"Invariably, parents say that they are fighting the case 'for the sake of the children', but in nine cases out of ten this is a lie. They are fighting each other using the children as pawns – a wretched situation. It destroys children perhaps for life to see their parents

> fight. My parents divorced over fifty years ago. I know
> that my sister and I are still damaged by their divorce
> and the aftermath. If you have children, strive for a
> damage limitation exercise."

Judge Christopher Compston (forty-six-year career in family law)

William

I was married for about seventeen years and I have two children, who now live with my ex. When things started to go wrong for us we had lots of discussions and I moved out for about two weeks. She then asked me to come back, which really cheered me up. We saw counsellors for about a year and even did The Marriage Course. We tried very hard to sort things out.

About two years later, a week after my father's death, I was stunned to receive a letter filing for divorce. That was a very painful time and, looking back, I didn't have time to grieve over my father's death because I became so caught up in the divorce. It was a horrible experience and I remember having a number of suicidal thoughts. I was doing a lot of work in Yorkshire, which meant driving there from London and back each day. It was dark, and I thought how easy it would be to end it all there and then. That's the sort of pain you go through. It's not a good way to think, but it happens.

I lived in the family home for a further year, even with the divorce in process, and it was very stressful and tense. Eventually I did move out but only just round the corner, so that I could still see the kids. Then, just two weeks after I had moved out, her new boyfriend moved in. While I'd suspected it a few months earlier, in a funny way I had chosen not to believe it, so it was a surprise when it happened.

How were you able to resolve your problems?

Communication issues were really important for me because we went through a very difficult financial divorce. We ended up in court for a whole day on the financial settlement, and it was such a bad experience – I wouldn't wish it on anyone. I came out of it in shock. I was still in shock that night in bed and my body felt as if it was in a different world.

Later, when the final court hearing was only two weeks away, I realized that I couldn't go through another court experience like that. Interestingly, this was around the same time as I did the session on Restored Lives on letting go and forgiving. I knew what I had to do. I picked up the phone and spoke directly to my ex. I had to talk to her and not leave it to the lawyers, because I couldn't bear losing many more thousands of pounds to them.

I made a choice to settle. I gave a lot away, but I felt total freedom in doing that. I knew it was right and I just had to trust that my children and I would be OK. I was able to let go irrespective of whether I felt it was just or unjust, and that was important for me. Actually making that choice also meant that I had started to forgive her.

Have I truly forgiven her? Yes, in many ways, but I have realized that it is something I have to keep working at over time. We have had lots of disagreements since we formally divorced, particularly over the kids. You have to take a positive decision to forgive because that's the only way to gain freedom. But it's the best form of self-interest, because when you are free, you are able to move on.

It's taken about three years of making that choice to forgive. Then other things come up: for example, at the moment I am finding it difficult because my wife remarried in June and the legal divorce was only finalized in January. I ask myself whether I have forgiven her new husband. He's got nothing to do with me but he came into my children's world, and that is hard. It's another stage in reaching forgiveness and it's not easy. I need strength to do it.

I am very positive now and believe that there are good plans and times ahead.

Where do I find a good lawyer?

"So I'm thinking of getting a divorce – the first thing that I have to do is to find a good lawyer, right?" **STOP! WAIT!**

Signing up a lawyer is not the first thing you need to do when you are thinking of separating – this is a common misconception. The most important starting point is to understand the problems you have to resolve and the options available for you to do this.

Resolving the issues that have legal consequences does not need to become World War III. In essence, it is all about communication and resolving conflict, and therefore the tools outlined in Chapters 3 and 4 are vital in this process.

It is important to keep your mind fixed on this fact. You can choose to bring in extra help and input from someone else, such as a lawyer or a mediator, in the way that best meets your needs.

Sometimes the best person to help you sort these things out is someone who can facilitate communication between you and enable the two of you to arrive at a mutually acceptable solution. This could be a mutual friend or a professional mediator, but it doesn't have to be a lawyer. Lord Wilson, one of the UK's senior family law judges, said this:

> *When we face serious family problems, we still usually say to ourselves, "I must find a solicitor." But in many (though not all) cases, we would do better to say, "We must find a mediator."*
>
> See http://www.thefma.co.uk/lj_wilson

Finding a mediator may well be the best way of starting to resolve your legal problems, and this method of conflict resolution is being used more and more.

Let's look first at the legal aspects and the options available to you, and then you can choose whom you need to help you.

What do we need to sort out?

In the midst of the gathering storm of a relationship breakdown there are so many things to sort out. When a separation process is initiated it's vital to stand back and be clear about which disputes may need third-party support to help resolve them.

The aspects to focus on are the ones that require both you *and* your ex to agree on a solution together. Some of these may be immediate concerns and others will be longer-term matters. I have highlighted below the normal short-term issues that need to be resolved once a separation has started, and which are relevant irrespective of the laws relating to your area.

Short-term concerns

- How will life continue from day to day?
- Are we going to be living in the same house for the time being? If so, how are we going to be able to do this?
- How are the bills going to be paid?
- Where will the children live?
- How and when will both parents see the children?
- Do we need external help to enable us to talk better and sort out practical matters?
- When and how will we think about whether we can stay together as a couple?

These short-term things may need to be agreed between you and your ex on a temporary basis until the longer-term issues have been resolved.

Longer-term concerns

The longer-term issues require more careful thought about how you will resolve them:

1. **The marriage** – in nearly all countries, a marriage has legal standing and the formal legal ending of this union is the divorce.

2. **The money** – this includes dividing the property, pensions, assets, investments, and income as well as any ongoing payments to each other or for taking care of children.

3. **The children's needs** – on a practical level children need housing, education, and financial support, and both parents have a responsibility to provide this. On an emotional level, they have a right to enjoy a relationship with both parents and they need emotional security during what may be a turbulent time for their parents.

Personal exercise

List your specific short-term and long-term concerns and issues.

Regardless of what country you live in and which particular law covers your situation, there are some universal principles that provide a helpful starting place for resolving your disputes.

Universal principles

HOW YOU NEGOTIATE THE ISSUES IS KEY TO YOUR ONGOING RELATIONSHIP AND YOUR OWN RECOVERY

The way that you resolve your problems will dictate how you communicate together in the future. If you choose to be constructive in the way you talk with your ex, this will be the platform from which you start to build your future contact with them.

If hatred is allowed to fester and revenge is plotted through a wall of lawyers (with you and your ex in the background), then recovery will take longer and your new life will be delayed.

Choosing to resolve disputes in a constructive manner will save you time, money, and stress and will help rebuild your self-confidence.

IF YOU HAVE CHILDREN, THE NATURE OF YOUR ONGOING RELATIONSHIP IS VITAL

However your own issues are resolved, parents need an ongoing relationship together which will shape their children's lives. To ensure that the impact of your divorce on your children is minimized, you should seek the least heated and least confrontational way of resolving your differences. This will mean putting the children's needs first, and viewing them as the most important factor as you arrive at your solutions.

A confrontational legal divorce process may end all hope of an amicable parenting relationship and will detract from your future relationship with the children.

What happens if the legal process goes badly?

The process that you choose can have huge consequences both for your life now, and for how you live in the future. This is when things can really go seriously wrong (yes, even worse than when you broke up).

The consequences are not just in terms of your relationship with your ex, but also in terms of your physical and mental health, as the stress involved in a confrontational legal battle can scar you for a lifetime and sometimes even longer! The story of the actor Dennis Hopper and his ex-wife, Victoria Duffy, highlight this "after-death" continuation and is a good example of how people can use the law courts to express their anger and bitterness:

> In January 2010, the actor Dennis Hopper made headlines when he filed to divorce his estranged wife, Victoria Duffy, while on his deathbed. Hopper died in May 2010 but found time up till then to have a bitter divorce battle with numerous arguments over various shared items, including sculptures by Robert Graham and Banksy, and a portrait by Andy Warhol.
>
> The battle continued after Hopper's death, with Duffy filling a lawsuit against Hopper's Trust, demanding that her exercise bike, butcher's block, juicer, rosebushes, and even asparagus tongs be returned to her.

The legal process is a bad place to vent your anger and try to gain revenge. It is stressful and costly in time and money, and the outcome is far from guaranteed.

The legal process in most countries does not aim to punish a "guilty" party and seek justice for the "victim". It is purely about resolving the legal responsibilities and practical consequences that arise when a relationship breaks down. It is not about getting "justice" in the broader sense even though that may be what you are hoping for.

What should our attitude be?

> *Don't let the legal process dictate your attitude; make your attitude dictate the process.*

The best thing to take into resolving your disputes is a positive, constructive approach. This is a balance between seeking good communication while taking a firm stance on the aspects that mean the most to you. If this seems impossible, then get some personal support in the form of friends or counselling. Try not to let your emotional distress colour a sensible approach to the legal issues.

These are some helpful goals to set yourself and anyone who is helping you:

- Be polite in tone and not aggressive or rude.

- Make sure that you retain the ability to have direct communication with your ex.

- Seek to overcome mistrust and misunderstanding with calm questions and a readiness to listen to answers.

- Seek to build good communications at every stage.

- Be persistent and patient.

- Prioritize the children's needs and interests above your own.

- Seek a reasonable financial settlement *in the light of the resources available.*

Having these goals and a positive, constructive attitude does *not* mean that you will be weak in negotiations. It is perfectly possible to take a strong, consistent position to protect your own interests in a dispute while maintaining a wholly constructive approach.

This attitude will help everyone to focus on the end goal, which is to find a fair way forward and to begin a new, fresh life separate from each other but having a good working relationship with each other as parents. A constructive approach to your ex will not only help your children but will also help you in the long run and speed up your recovery.

Options for resolving disputes

There are a number of options for how to deal with the longer-term matters that need to be settled (these being the divorce, money, and children). The route that you take will have an enormous effect on your own health, wealth, and recovery, as well as on your children's well-being.

The diagram below sets out the various options for resolving these issues. These options are common across the UK, USA, Canada, Australia, New Zealand, and many other countries around the world. The way that they are implemented may vary slightly, depending on your particular state or country, and it's therefore helpful to research the particular points that are relevant to your circumstance. There are numerous excellent websites explaining the legal process, some operated by law firms and others run independently.

It is important to recognize that only one of these long-term issues automatically requires a legal document to be completed – that is the legal ending of a marriage. For children or finances you may or may not need to frame your agreed solution in a legal document, depending on which country you are in.

Options diagram

The diagram below highlights the decision-making process for each option.

Options for resolving legal issues

Working together to agree solutions

1. Around a kitchen table
2. Discussions with a friend
3. Mediation
4. Collaborative law

Cheaper, quicker, empowering, builds relationships

- -

Working against each other – attack and defence

5. Solicitors and court proceedings
(Barristers, court hearings, decision by judge)

Costly, takes longer, more stressful, destroys relationships

For options above the dotted line, control and choice remain in your hands and there is more potential for building communication between the two of you. For the options below the dotted line of the diagram, control and choice move into the hands of outsiders, ultimately a court. In this situation, with representatives between you and your ex, there is much more likelihood of communication difficulty and increasing cost.

1. AROUND A KITCHEN TABLE

At the top is the simplest process, in which the two of you sit together and work all the issues out. For couples who are still communicating and feel comfortable discussing things together, this can be a good route, especially if the financial situation is not complex and they have agreed on the arrangements for children. If there is uncertainty over a particular aspect, which requires input from a financial adviser or lawyer, then the couple can take advice separately and come back to the table to agree on what to do.

Some couples use internet sites to process their legal divorce online to keep the cost to a minimum. This can be helpful in cases that are very simple and have no detailed financial aspects. If you use the internet do check whether you receive independent legal advice, as without this your agreement may not be legally binding.

Any agreement made at the kitchen table or over the internet (particularly a financial one) can if necessary be taken to a lawyer to be made into a legally binding contract between the two.

For many couples this route is impractical, as communication has broken down or trust been lost to such a degree that external support is needed to enable both parties to come to a reasonable agreement.

2. DISCUSSIONS WITH A FRIEND

Additional support can be given by inviting a mutually trusted friend to help you reach a solution (illustrated in the next level down on the diagram). This friend is there to help facilitate the discussion between you.

Again, any specific questions relating to a particular financial matter or legal point can be taken to a professional.

Specific answers can then be brought back into the discussion and agreed, with any final solution being written up by a lawyer in a legally binding contract if necessary.

3. MEDIATION

The next level is mediation. Mediation is not marriage counselling; it is when a professionally trained facilitator guides and supports couples in discussing matters and helps them to find their own solutions.

The mediator **can give information** to both of you about legal matters but **will not give any advice**, as their role is to remain neutral between the parties throughout. Therefore a mediator can give information about the legal requirements for a divorce, the factors that a court will take into consideration when making a financial settlement, or the documents that need to be filed. Mediators cannot, for instance, advise one person on what is reasonable for them to accept as a financial settlement.

What mediators will do is help you both listen to each other and identify what is most important to each of you, thereby enabling you to work together to arrive at the best outcome for you and the family. There is a focus on rebuilding and restoring a couple's confidence in resolving disputes. All the options can be explored in a totally confidential environment and, because the couple have found their own solution, any agreement is much more likely to be respected and implemented.

Rebuilding a couple's ability to communicate is a vital part of this process because life will change in the future and new areas of potential dispute will arise. The ability to resolve these issues quickly, rather than going back to court each time, will enable you to rebuild your life much faster.

USING LEGAL ADVICE DURING A MEDIATION PROCESS

If important legal matters are being discussed, it is vital that mediation should go hand-in-hand with obtaining your own independent legal advice.

At any stage during mediation, a client can get advice from a lawyer on what is reasonable for them in their particular circumstances, and can then come back to mediation better informed and ready to reach agreement. Mediation does not replace legal advice; it works best when lawyers are in the background advising the couple, and this facilitates an efficient and cost-effective process.

Example: Using a lawyer to advise you on a reasonable or likely financial settlement

In some countries the financial settlement is not fixed but depends on a number of variables that a court believes are fair and relevant. A mediator can guide you on which of the variables would be most important in your circumstances. However, because they cannot advise you, this may be a moment to take specific advice from a lawyer on their assessment of the outcome for you if you were to go to court and have a judge decide on your case.

Once all the information relating to your financial position has been collected, a lawyer can advise you on the upper and lower level of a financial settlement that a court would probably arrive at. A range is necessary because the outcome of any court judgment is uncertain, as different factors may be regarded as more important by different judges. The upper level is the best settlement from the most favourable judge. The lower level is the worst settlement from the least favourable judge.

All being well, with the same financial information, the two of you will obtain relatively similar ranges from your lawyers, which you can then take back into the mediation meetings to negotiate an agreement.

Problems will obviously arise if different financial information is given to the lawyers. This would result in different estimates being given to each person of the likely financial settlement. The way to resolve this is through more detailed investigation of the exact financial position, before discussions can resume and a settlement be agreed.

As with the chats around the kitchen table or with the help of a trusted friend, the decision-making in mediation rests entirely with the clients. The benefit of mediation is that it provides a better way of building communication and resolving the legal, financial, and children's issues with your ex directly.

The difference between mediators and lawyers

Mediators are trained to enable couples to talk to each other and find solutions that work for them both. Their skill is in conflict resolution. They gather the relevant facts (regarding the children or financial details) and help the couple explore options for an agreed solution. The outcome is decided by the couple, not the mediator.

Lawyers, on the other hand, are there to defend the interests of their client (that's you). Other priorities, such as looking at the long-term needs of your children or protecting your ability to communicate with your ex, are not included within their standard brief. A bad lawyer will fuel the fire of mistrust, fear, and bitterness early in the process and so, if you are employing a lawyer, ensure that they communicate in a way that is constructive and, as far as possible, non-adversarial.

The truth of many legal disputes about children is that a parent may "win the battle but lose the war". For example, you might win the argument about where a child sleeps on a Friday night but in so doing destroy any remaining goodwill with the other parent. The destruction of the parenting relationship will have a long-lasting detrimental effect on the child, worse than any short-term dispute over Friday nights. This type of dispute is best handled sensitively and constructively and not be left to the sledgehammer system that is the experience of many through the court processes.

4. COLLABORATIVE LAW

Many countries have introduced an option called collaborative law as a helpful alternative. This aims to avoid the expensive court process while providing clients with more substantial legal help.

Collaborative law follows a similar format to mediation, whereby the matters at hand are dealt with by the clients sitting round a table. However, instead of using a neutral mediator, each person has a solicitor representing them who commits, together with the couple, to resolving the issues without going to court.

Mediation is ideal for many, but there are some people who do not feel able to conduct negotiations directly with their spouse without their own legal adviser being present. For example, it can be reassuring to have a solicitor present at the discussions if one person is very domineering or controlling, or if one person feels out of their depth or lacking in confidence.

If no agreement is reached, then the only alternative is to refer the case to more lawyers and the courts, as collaborative law lawyers are not allowed to represent you in any court proceedings. This means there is a huge incentive for both sides to reach agreement to prevent a waste of time and money.

Collaborative law is more expensive than mediation but is still much less costly and lengthy than a court case. As with mediation, the process is led by the clients and the decision-making rests with them.

5. REPRESENTATION BY SOLICITORS

Many people are unaware of the options discussed so far and assume that the traditional lawyer and court process is the only way forward. Maybe this is also because the public tend to be aware of the most heated and contested divorce cases, which are reported in the press, or the intensive advertising of law firms.

A good solicitor will advise you of the alternative options of mediation or collaborative law. If those processes are not chosen, then the issues will be addressed by the lawyers writing letters to each other, and by court proceedings.

There are some excellent solicitors who will work at finding a settlement for you, but there are others who will simply let the court proceedings take their course. In the latter case, there are usually no face-to-face meetings other than those that happen in court, with all the stress and fear that goes with that.

Many cases are settled before a final court hearing and judgment, but, if this doesn't happen, the case is heard by a judge and a decision imposed by means of a court order. In the UK, the process of resolving finances takes many months (usually well over a year). Disputes over arrangements for children can take several months. Either way, a court case will involve a huge cost to you – in time, money, and stress.

In some extreme cases a lawyer and court process is inevitable, for instance those involving severe abuse, financial fraud, child protection issues, addiction, or mental illness. In these situations, neither mediation nor collaborative law is appropriate and the court route is the only option, but these situations are unusual.

Summary of the available options

Overall, the options available above the dotted line in the diagram are very different from the one below it. Above the line, you decide what should happen, it is quicker, it is cheaper, it is less stressful (as you control the outcome), and it can rebuild communication between you and your ex. Below the line, the outcome is increasingly left to others as you proceed further along the court route. If you cannot agree before a court hearing then a judge will decide your fate as part of a process that is expensive, time-consuming, and stressful. It will also worsen the communication between the two of you, which may take years to regain and will impede your recovery and impact your children.

That is why, in many circumstances, it is wise to call in a mediator first. Do you want to rebuild communication to get to a solution, or be further separated by taking defensive positions? Even if you do not have children, using a mediator gives you the opportunity to facilitate a mutually acceptable solution more quickly and at a lower cost than using a lawyer and a court process. It gives you the opportunity to recover in a faster and healthier fashion.

How do you choose the right process with your ex?

Agree on the right process before employing anyone. Obviously talk to mediators, lawyers, and friends before coming to your conclusion, but don't "sign up" a professional before agreeing the route with your ex. There is often a degree of tension and mistrust at this stage and this can make people default to the route of lawyers and court processes, simply because you assume that this "protects your interests" most. This is untrue – your interests can be protected just as well above the dotted line as below; however, above the line the process may also enhance your journey of recovery.

It is therefore wise, at the earliest possible point, to have a discussion with your ex about the option you believe will work best for you as a couple. Maybe use this chapter as the basis for your discussions. Show it to your ex so that he or she can also have an unbiased view of the options available. Any of the above-the-line options are dependent on both of you agreeing to it – it is not a choice you can make on your own.

It is not always possible to agree on the process with your ex. If one person has already hired a top lawyer to defend them, it can be difficult to back down and you may then feel you need to fight back with a similar lawyer. If you have proceeded down one route and now believe that it is not helping you, an alternative is to put everyone "on pause" while you both try a different route, such as mediation. If this doesn't work then you can always go back to the lawyers. Mediation can be used at any stage along the way.

Personal exercise

Which option do you want to take? Which option do you think your ex would like to take?

When the legal divorce arrives

The day that the legal divorce arrives can bring with it a number of different feelings depending on your situation.

The process of receiving the final legal papers can seem very surreal and detached for something that is so significant. In addition, the legal divorce often comes many months after the key choices about the relationship have been made, and so your thoughts and feelings may have changed substantially during that period.

For some people, it brings an end to a sad chapter and may raise all those unhappy emotions once again. However, others may want to mark this event in some way to help them to focus on the future and a new stage of their life.

It may be difficult to contemplate how you will feel, but it may be helpful to think ahead to enable you to prepare yourself as much as you can.

Helen (lawyer and mediator)

As a solicitor I originally trained in family law and spent several years working with clients to sort out their financial disputes and disagreements about their children following relationship breakdown. This involved corresponding with the ex's lawyers and managing court proceedings on my client's behalf. I quickly realized that the most constructive way to help my clients resolve issues was to get them around a table to talk things through. Even in non-acrimonious cases, it's easy to pick up a negative impression of the other spouse and these joint meetings would be the first time I would meet the ex and hear their side of the story.

As a solicitor, I was being paid to defend my client's position against their ex, either in a round-the-table meeting, or in correspondence, or in court. My job was to protect my client's financial position and achieve the best possible outcome for them. However much I tried to be constructive in my communications with the other side, it was inevitably an adversarial and confrontational process, as that was what I was being paid for.

I took several years out when I had my own children and, as I began to think about returning to work, I felt sick at the idea of going back into that adversarial process to argue in disputes, especially child-related ones. As a parent myself, I had become more aware of a child's basic need to have parents who can function effectively as parents, and not fight. So, instead of returning to litigation, I trained as a mediator, and have not looked back!

The first dramatic difference was that I had to get used to meeting both clients at the outset, not just one. It made me realize how biased I used to be as a solicitor, always hearing from one side only. The new objectivity was refreshing and very helpful in understanding the conflict between the clients better.

Secondly, it was exhilarating not to be defending a position, but to be able to work constructively with both clients to find out what really mattered to them. In many cases it was the children who were most important and I helped the clients to look at how they could both fulfil their parental responsibility to meet their children's needs. Compared with the defended adversarial approach that I had had to take as a solicitor, it is so much more constructive to be working alongside clients as a mediator.

One case I had really sums up the difference.

The parents of a five-year-old boy had been living in the UK for several years but were now divorcing. The husband's work was in the UK but the wife was keen to go back to her home abroad to her family, friends, and her in-laws, with whom she was still on good terms. She needed the father's consent to move the son permanently away from the UK. He refused and – thankfully – they came to mediation before either of them had spoken to lawyers.

In the first session, we helped them discuss what a father's role should be for a son (as that was the role that would be compromised if the son left the UK). In the course of that discussion, the wife vented her irritation and hurt at what she said were his failings as a father. Her son would lose very little by emigrating away from him. He said he would have loved to be more involved but he hadn't wanted to hassle her as he'd hurt her so much when he left her. It was quite an emotional exchange.

They came back a few weeks later. She said that he'd been fantastic since the last session and was doing so much more with the boy, so much so, that she was now concerned about whether it was right for her to go. He said he had loved spending time with his son but it had also given him a better understanding of her life, and he didn't feel that it was right to stop her going back to where she came from!

We had quite a discussion and, in the end, they agreed that she would go but that they would spend a lot of time together with their son before they left. He would drive them to the airport so that the boy knew he was not being taken away from his father against his wishes. They also had a detailed programme of phone calls on Skype and future visits planned, with the mother fully recognizing and supporting the important role played by the father in her son's life.

Had they been to solicitors first, she would have been advised that she had a strong case and that he had little chance of stopping her. Any lawyer involvement would have led to expense, delay (a court case would have taken many months), and stress. But, more significantly, their move abroad would have been against the father's will. This would have destroyed their already strained relationship as parents. Who knows how that boy's relationship with his father would have deteriorated?

Mediation provided a totally different outcome for both the child and his parents, which was cheap and quick and enabled them to arrive at a solution on good terms with each other. I love my mediation work so much more than acting as a solicitor.

TOOLBOX TO TAKE AWAY
Sorting out the legal matters

Don't just sign up a lawyer – list your short- and long-term concerns and the options available

The communication and conflict resolution tools are important here

Universal principles:

- *How you negotiate is key to your ongoing relationship and your own recovery.*
- *If you have children, the nature of your ongoing relationship is vital.*

Venting your anger and taking revenge through lawyers is costly and doomed to failure

Take a positive, constructive attitude into your negotiations and set clear goals

Understand the options available for resolving your legal issues – what are the alternatives to a court process?

A professional mediator is often a good option to choose – assess what's best for you and your ex

Try to reach agreement with your ex on the "process" before tackling any issues to be resolved

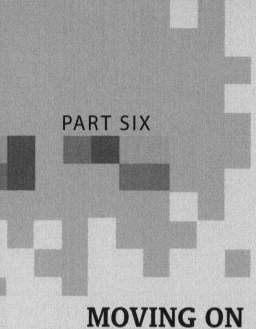

PART SIX

MOVING ON

Chapter 10

Being single and moving forward

Recovery is:

"Enjoying new experiences and friendships without my past experiences draining the fun away. When the question 'What next?' becomes exciting rather than overwhelming."

Hannah

"Not longing for a relationship but feeling happy with yourself."

John

"Being able to smile again and talk about my marriage without getting upset."

Dean

"Noticing you're laughing – a real belly laugh."

Amy

"Relationship breakdown is a bit like childbirth. The approaching separation is terrifying. It was probably the most painful experience in my life, and afterwards such a relief to get through to the other side."

Jan

"Looking forward and forgetting all that went before – recovery is a breath of fresh air. It's like being in a new land, and it's exciting!"

Jenica

The beginning of a new life is painful. Childbirth often brings tremendous pain, but soon the pain is forgotten and you start to look forward with hope. Starting a new life after a relationship breakdown has many similarities, with a lot of pain and hurt. Having seen many, many people get through their relationship breakdown, I can tell you that, if you have to take this path, there is hope and excitement to come.

Of course you can't expect to move from one life to another in one quick leap, and you will probably experience a series of successes and failures. If you feel stuck in a rut or see yourself as a failure most of the time, find someone to talk to about it. Go on a divorce recovery course or speak to a doctor or a counsellor, especially if you have been feeling low for a while.

Taking responsibility for the future

During separation, we tend to look both backwards and inwards, which makes moving forward impossible. However, there comes a moment when we can take full responsibility for our future. This is when we can start to feel our confidence increase and see some light at the end of our dark tunnel.

Karina tells of the moment when she realized this:

A real turning point came for me when I realized that a lot of the moving forward was up to me and that I had to take responsibility for myself and for my part in the relationship breakdown.

It came after I had been separated for a number of months and the kids and I were rushing out of the house, late for school and for

work (which I was only doing because he had gone!). We found that
some foxes had attacked our bins and the rubbish was all over the
front of the house. As I tidied up the mess I was in tears and found
myself saying to the kids, "This wouldn't have happened if Daddy
was here."

I realized that I was blaming him for the foxes attacking our bins
and, in fact, for everything bad in my life. I realized then how angry
I was, and knew that I had to stop holding everything against him
and let it go.

As Karina found, there comes a moment when we can begin to take responsibility for our own life rather than looking back and blaming others for all our current circumstances. We have to take responsibility for the choices we make now, which will shape our future.

At that moment, we become positive when we ask forward-looking questions such as, "What shall I do on Saturdays?"; "How do I go to a party on my own?"; "What shall I do about a holiday?" or "How shall I celebrate my birthday?"

This is when the question "What next?" becomes exciting rather than overwhelming. Facing these questions with a positive attitude will help bring recovery and mean that we can start the next, improved, chapter of our life.

Below are some responses from divorced and separated people to the question: "What does recovery look like for you?"

- Being thankful for where I am and looking forward to the adventure of life.

- Not caring or being worried when meeting the new "you" in your ex's life.

- Learning to take better care of myself and let go of the need to fix things.

- It's an ongoing process – I have good days and bad days. The most important thing is to stay positive and keep going. Be kind to yourself. Love yourself.

- Getting back in touch with my feelings, examining my own heart, and being honest with myself. A new chapter of my life has begun!

- It's about discovering the new you. The best place to build new foundations is rock bottom.

- An opportunity to confront the past, learn from mistakes and face the future with hope and optimism.

- It's a better relationship with my son.

- It's learning that forgiveness is a decision, not a feeling.

- It's a confidence that I am wiser and more mature than before, more tolerant and accepting, and more able to recognize my own weaknesses and strengths.

- Being free from the past and not feeling the pain.

- Being joyful and embracing life.

- Laughing again and being at peace.

- Freedom, independence, happiness, and faith in the future.

Moving on

If you are already divorced, some of this chapter may not be relevant. Skim through it but don't miss the section on "Signing off with your ex" towards the end, as it is relevant for everyone.

However, if you are still married, a key part of moving on is answering the question "Is the marriage really over?" This is such an important question for us to answer, as it enables us to move on more successfully.

I have heard many people say that a sharp dispute can quickly become more serious and lead to separation and divorce proceedings. You rapidly feel out of control and start heading towards being single without knowing what has hit you.

If you are not yet legally divorced, may I encourage you to pause and think: "Is this really what I want?"; "Is there anything more I can do to prevent it?"

> In my case, Karen was pushing for a divorce and the proceedings were moving ahead quickly. I put them on hold to ask Karen whether it was really what we wanted. This was hard to do because I knew that it would take a lot of effort from both sides to restore our relationship. However, I wanted to be able to look back and say I had done everything I could to make this marriage work; after all, I had promised to do this through good times and bad.
>
> What I did was to write to Karen a letter and ask her to reconsider. In the end she didn't want to, but it helped me greatly to look back and say that I had done everything I could. I would encourage you to pause and see whether there is anything you can do to prevent divorce.

Obviously it takes two people to make a relationship work; however, it's important to face this question individually. It's vital that you yourself answer it truthfully, and I have therefore set out five areas, each with a question, that will help you to clarify your answer.

1. Be honest about your feelings and don't make big decisions when highly emotional

You need to be honest with yourself about your underlying feelings. More recent emotions such as anger can colour the way you look at good experiences from the past.

When you are angry and "see red", that's all you can see. If you are feeling highly emotional, it is the wrong time to think about key long-term questions about life.

> *I knew of one person who was in the midst of a difficult separation and court case. He was desperate to ensure he never made the same mistakes again, so much so that he was planning to have an operation to prevent him from having kids. It was the wrong time to make this significant life choice.*

Be patient and don't be pushed into anything quickly. Take some time to allow your highly charged emotions to cool and then think it through carefully.

Question: *Have you allowed enough time for your emotions to calm down?*

2. Recognize the significance and depth of marriage

It is helpful to recognize the significance and depth of a marriage relationship – this isn't a casual friendship. A marriage is a public declaration of commitment between two people, reinforced by strong vows and promises. The breaking of these promises is significant – more like an amputation than minor surgery.

This is why some people say it takes three to five years to recover from the average marriage breakdown. Taking, say, six months of your life to focus your time and money on rebuilding your current relationship may be the best thing to do.

Question: *Have you carefully assessed the consequences of a divorce and the benefits of investing some time and money in rebuilding what you already have?*

3. Understand what it takes to make a relationship work

Luck and finding the perfect partner are not the key ingredients of a good relationship. There *are* no "perfect partners", as I have come to realize through finding out how far I am from being perfect!

Similarly, I have also often wondered why it is that "opposites attract" when our differences can later become the very things that threaten to push us away from each other.

We need to consider thoughtfully what really makes relationships work.

> It was only after my own relationship broke down that I started investigating what makes them work. That reflects badly on me, but fortunately there are years of experience out there in many good books and relationship resources that can help you.

If we all had to pass a test on how to make relationships work, much as we have to get a licence to drive a car, there would be a lot fewer relationship crashes! Relationships are obviously much more complicated than driving a car, but, if we don't understand what makes a relationship work, we are unlikely to have success in them. Therefore, we do well to find out what creates a good relationship and discover our own strengths and weaknesses in that area.

Question: *How would you discover the key ways to create a good relationship?*

4. Small changes can make big differences

I have seen many cases in which a couple feel exhausted and devoid of hope that they can resolve the conflicts in their marriage. However, with the inspiration of some outside help, such as a good marriage course or counsellor, a small change has started a process that turns the tide of emotions in the other direction. When the couple have children or a significant mutual history, the tide can turn quickly because their marriage bond is very close.

If there is a willingness to try, then there is usually a way to make the relationship work again, because one positive change on the part of one person can make this tide turn.

Question: Are there some small changes that you could try in conjunction with some outside support?

5. Recognize your own mistakes and say sorry

Recognize the things that you have not done well in your relationship, and apologize for them. Forgiving and letting go is so much easier if someone has said sorry, and this can quickly open the door to a fresh, renewed relationship.

Question: Is there anything that you could have done better? Are you able to say sorry?

Take time to go through these questions and maybe come back to them to make sure you are clear about and satisfied with your answers.

You should think carefully about what you can do to make your relationship work. However, not all relationships will continue, and you must be careful not to tolerate unacceptable behaviour, such as abuse or other situations where you should get outside help quickly.

What do you need if you hope to re-establish your marriage?

If you have hopes of re-establishing your marriage relationship, I have some pointers to guide you through the next steps.

If you are both willing to try (even if each of you has only a very small hope), then it is vital to invest some time and money in giving your relationship your best shot.

Participating in a structured course such as The Marriage Course, and seeing a good counsellor at the same time, will help you to unlock the key issues and start building a healthier relationship. Many people have found this to be an effective way of rebuilding a marriage. They learn how to make relationships work and how to change unhealthy habits.

If only one of you has this hope, then it is of course much harder to succeed. It takes two to make a relationship work and therefore you will have to be extremely patient, giving your partner sufficient emotional space to be able to make their own decision. These are some ground rules that will help you:

1. Get support. I would encourage you to make sure that you have good personal support. It is difficult to hope for marital reconciliation while you see no improvement. During a separation it is vital to have someone close to you who can give you wise, sensible advice – not necessarily always agreeing with you, but being a good sounding board. Consider whether seeing a counsellor will help you.

2. Make sure that you start by building normal, polite, and friendly relations with your ex. This is a vital first step.

3. Affairs or other close third-party relationships need to end before you can have any hope of a sensible discussion on re-establishing your relationship. Don't do anything until these have finished.

4. Things will need to change. You need to view any marital reconciliation as you would a new relationship – you will both need to change some of the ways in which you relate to each other to make it work.

5. Ensure that your life is not completely "on hold" – find a new activity or something that you really enjoy, which can build you up and give you confidence.

6. You are the only person who can judge how long you should "wait" for your partner and maintain hope that your relationship can restart. Your friends and family may quickly say "Move on", but if you still have hope then that is the most important factor.

Signing off with your ex

If these efforts do not work and you do arrive at a legal divorce, an important step in being able to move on successfully is signing off with your ex in a good way.

To some of you this may sound like a crazy idea, as you don't need to talk to your ex and you really don't want to. But don't switch off! Everything here is for *your* benefit alone.

The reason this is of benefit to you is that if you can have sensible, pleasant, civil relations with your ex, then you are in a far better position to move on successfully in your life.

If you have a continuing relationship, such as parenting children together, then it is vital to be able to talk to each other without getting angry or frustrated every time. But, even if you don't have a continuing relationship, the ability to wish your ex well for the future will help you to obtain a sense of closure and enable you not to fear meeting them in the future.

For my part, I am amazed at how much thinking time has been taken up by the idea of bumping into Karen, even though we didn't have any reason or likelihood of meeting up. She has very blond hair, so I found myself constantly looking at people with blond hair in the street, wondering whether it was her. What a waste of time and energy! The chances of meeting her were minuscule, but I still used to think about it a lot! Why was I doing this when I had completely forgiven her?

The way to counteract this fear is to sign off on a good note. After everything is finished, try to have some contact of a friendly nature and "wish them well". If you have wished your ex well the last time you spoke, then the next time you meet (if you ever do) you can continue the conversation much more easily.

> I didn't talk to Karen after the legal process had finished. In the end it was many years before I said to myself, "This is crazy! I'm spending so much time thinking about bumping into her." I decided to contact her and I wished her well in the future. It was an important step, as it meant I was no longer worried about meeting or bumping into her and had clearly acted out my forgiveness. I finished on a friendly note and it enabled me to move on. I wish I had done it earlier.

Wishing their ex well is possible only for people who have rebuilt their confidence.

For those who have had particularly difficult relationships, maybe involving abuse of some sort, it may be valid not to seek to do this for your own protection. However, it's a process that will help *you*, so keep it in mind if you are considering meeting your ex or planning to meet them soon.

Summary

A process of reflection on your marriage is an important part of your onward journey. If there is anything you can do to keep your marriage going, it's important to try. This is the story of Peter and Gill Drysdale, who found their twenty-seven-year marriage hanging by a thread, with Peter on the point of beginning divorce proceedings. This is their story.

> **Peter:** Gill and I started going out at university in Durham and we fell in love. We got engaged at Easter 1976 and married in August 1978.

Those first three years of marriage were really interesting and quite challenging – among other things. I was learning the craft of being a husband. Then Gill became pregnant. Ian was born in April 1982. He was a great joy to us.

Eventually I ended up training for teaching. Then our daughter Ruth was born (1983), and, though that was a happy year, there were some tough times too. Financially we were under a great deal of pressure. I was starting at the bottom of the ladder as a teacher, so my salary was modest. I had to teach at night school to try to supplement our income. That's probably when the cracks first started to appear. We bickered a lot and didn't share our feelings with each other.

Gill: *I think I'd gone into marriage with a very idealistic view – but it hadn't really worked out quite the way I'd hoped. It was an awful lot of hard work.*

Peter: *Time went on and money problems eased. Then, about fifteen years ago, I left teaching to join Barclays Bank. But we still had underlying marital problems. I'd have an emotional outburst and then we'd be quiet, but nothing would get resolved. Sometimes, when you've got kids, if things aren't right between you you've just got to cope. Soon after I'd started at Barclays my job took me away from home for days at a time. So we got used to not seeing much of each other and became more distant.*

Gill: *I didn't want to face the fact that our relationship wasn't how I had hoped it would be. Throughout all of it we'd remained really good friends but I'd got to the stage of thinking, "I know I really like Pete, but do I actually love him?"*

Peter: *We were friendly with each other, but as for being lovers and "in love" – not really. But rather than saying, "Can we change this?" I just accepted that that wasn't going to be part of our relationship* *and gave up trying to be romantic. In 2000 we bought a house in France to renovate. Gill, who was teaching at the time, was able to spend the summer there. So over the next three or four years we tended to be living apart for five or six weeks at a time.*

When Gill came home from France last October, she seemed quite distant and cold. I started saying to her that it would be better for us each to be on our own than to pretend to have a relationship. At that point Gill started voicing some things that perhaps had been there for years.

Gill: *I was thinking, "We've been married all these years and the kids have gone, so what's my role now?" In the end I actually said to Pete, "I'm not sure if I love you or if I've ever loved you."*

Peter: *That hurt the most and I thought, "Well, this is it, then." I had bought a book on divorce and started reading it. In December I was about to call the divorce lawyer. I thought, "I've still got twenty good years of my life left; it's better for us to have a fresh start."*

Gill: *I didn't want to give up without a big fight. We spoke to some friends who were about to go on The Marriage Course because people had recommended it to them. When they suggested the course to us, Pete was a bit reluctant because he thought we were over, but, as I said, I wasn't going to give up without a fight. So we started the course last April. The way it was all set up was beautiful. We had a meal and we talked. We couldn't argue because we were in public, but the background music meant that we knew we weren't going to be overheard.*

Peter: *I was still ambiguous for the first few sessions. There was a session on forgiveness. We'd hurt each other over the years and when we started identifying those times, and asking for forgiveness, that was extremely powerful.*

Gill: *It was a safe place for us to really talk about things. The whole course was definitely very emotional for us.*

Peter: *Although there were significant moments throughout the course, if we were asked to pick one out it would be during the "love languages" session. This is when you talk about expressing love in the way you need or want to be loved. There are a number of ways in which people express love, and if your partner does it differently from your preferred ways it's like speaking a different language to each other.*

I'd got it into my head that Gill didn't love me, and had never loved me, and on that evening we were asked to write down significant times when we'd felt loved. I thought, "I'm going to have a blank sheet of paper..." But then, when I started writing, memories came up of times when we'd supported and shared with each other. When we compared notes I was choking back tears, because I recognized that Gill had loved me all along. That was the moment when I knew our marriage was saved.

Gill: *That was the moment for me as well. I looked at our relationship and I suddenly thought, "Yes, I do actually love him." I think that Pete and I had loved each other all the time, but we hadn't realized it. Over the years we hadn't been looking after our love.*

Peter: *We both realized the significance of the moment straight away – it was so immediate and obvious – we knew our relationship had been saved. Ian and Ruth noticed it as well; they said they could see a change that same evening.*

Gill: *It was basically like falling in love again. When we went home, we weren't the same couple who had arrived earlier that evening.*

Peter: *My definition of love has changed completely — it's now about thinking about the other person. Love is about looking out for each other, and it's the greatest act of service.*

Gill: *We know how to talk to each other now, and how to listen.*

Peter: *We'd not given time to each other for years, so one huge difference is that every week we make sure we have time together. We've been on picnics, we've started going to art things, and we're jogging together.*

Gill: *We're both thinking, "Well, we love each other unconditionally, but we both want to change and be better, for ourselves and for the other person..."*

We know we'll have ups and downs and we'll argue, but in the end we can forgive each other and say sorry. We feel we are far stronger in our relationship now than we ever have been. We are so excited about our future now — I'm sure the next twenty-seven years are going to be better than the first twenty-seven.

Peter: *We're not there yet; we're not perfect. We had a disagreement recently, but what was different was that we talked about it and tried to listen to each other — the tools are there now.*

TOOLBOX TO TAKE AWAY
Being single and moving forward

Recovery is exciting. It's "freedom, independence, happiness and faith in the future"

Sign off on a good note — wish them well — it will help you to move on

Is the marriage really over?

- *Be honest about your feelings and don't make big decisions when highly emotional.*
- *Recognize the significance and depth of marriage.*
- *Understand what it takes to make a relationship work.*
- *Small changes can make big differences.*
- *Recognize your own mistakes and say sorry.*

Invest time and money in your relationship if you have any hope of re-establishing your marriage

Chapter 11

Building better relationships

"I stopped looking back and holding on to all that baggage of hate, anger, resentment, and bitterness – all the things that were basically defining me at the time. I started feeling hope and asking who I really was. Frankly I'd lost myself and had absolutely no idea who I was. Looking back on it now, it's the best thing that's happened to me…

"This is a good yardstick for how far I've got in my recovery – my best friend got married last August and he gave me the honour of being his best man, while at the same time my ex was chief bridesmaid. I was able to look up the aisle at my ex walking down it and be reminded of our marriage but still have peace in my heart. That was a massive gauge for me of my level of forgiveness and healing. There is hope now."

Robert

A vital part of recovery and moving on is having the skills and the confidence to build strong, meaningful relationships. These relationships, with people in every area of life, help you to focus on the future and give you meaning and purpose.

They can come in many different shapes and sizes: with family, friends, and children; at school, at work, with neighbours; and even with your ex.

I am going to look at the skills that make these relationships work, but, before I do this, a word of warning: beware of getting into intimate relationships – they are not the solution to your problems.

Intimate relationships

When you are recovering from a relationship breakdown, your self-esteem can be low and you are likely to be more vulnerable than usual. Getting into another intimate relationship may appear reassuring and make you feel loveable and attractive. Many people hope that it will blot out past rejection or fill the void left at the end of a relationship.

But a new intimate relationship is not a quick fix that will heal the pain inside you. If you ever felt used or rejected during your marriage, be aware that sleeping with someone else can leave you feeling even worse.

People sometimes get into another relationship quickly after a divorce and then find themselves completely at a loss when that relationship also fails. All the problems that have not been tackled in the past bubble up to the surface again and mix in with any issues from the latest relationship.

So it's important to talk about sex here, because it can be very difficult being celibate when you are newly single. Everyone has sexual feelings – the issue is deciding what to do about them. It's no good just taking a cold shower and ignoring the problem!

This is what Robert said (his full story is at the end of the chapter):

I separated from my ex and got into a relationship about five minutes afterwards. I had all this love to give, so I said, "Here, I'll give it to you." I threw myself into other relationships but it wasn't helpful; they were doomed from the start.

It took about three years for me genuinely to get over my ex, and my relationships after separation didn't help. I wish someone had told me beforehand that it was a bad idea. I went through a succession of relationships but all I learned was that I was not yet able to commit to anyone. I wanted affection and intimacy. Like everyone, I wanted to both feel and express love.

Around that time I also started mucking about with pornography on the internet, and it started to take over. It was only recently that I realized I was addicted to it. So I can state with some authority that it's really unhelpful — unhelpful for your own well-being. Do other things rather than immerse yourself in porn.

The problem was that I desperately longed for intimacy so as not to feel alone. I felt so terribly lonely because I had always been with someone, and that was how I got my affirmation, how I got love — I'm a red-blooded male, after all! After my third serious relationship ended I had ten months on my own. I realized that I'd not been single since I was eighteen, and all I'd been doing since amounted to putting a plaster on the big wound on my heart. I'd always been in a relationship and, if it broke up, I'd instantly get into another one so that I wouldn't have to deal with the pain.

What happened next was that I began to peel off all those plasters I'd applied, and it hurt like heck, but it was great. It was only when I gave up sex and relationships that I actually started to heal. I didn't become a saint overnight: giving up sex took a bit longer than that, but eventually it did happen.

After ten months I genuinely felt for the first time in my adult life that I wasn't on the rebound and I wasn't hurting. It was a really healthy thing for me.

It's hard not being in a sexual relationship any more, so what can you do? Here are some ideas:

- You need to channel your sexual feelings into other activities – it *is* possible to have a fulfilling life without a sexual relationship. For some people, it helps to pour their energies into new activities or work opportunities – giving them the sense that they are building for the future.

- For some single people, close friends are a great compensation for the lack of a sexual partner. You can have truly warm, affectionate, and intimate non-sexual relationships with good friends.

- Stay away from temptation. This may involve avoiding sexually explicit films and the internet, which give a short-term high but a long-term low. It will involve ignoring those films, books, and magazines that make you dissatisfied with your own life. It's like being on a diet – it's just not helpful to gaze longingly into the baker's window when it's full of cream cakes!

- Find someone to whom you can be accountable – someone who will ask at regular intervals how you're getting on with this area of your life. Like a weekly weigh-in at WeightWatchers®, this kind of accountability can help to keep you focused on your own recovery.

Build strong foundations

This is a vital stage in your life's journey. When change happens, it allows room for new growth, but it's up to you what form this growth is going to take.

By understanding your emotions and pinpointing the problem areas in your life, you can make the choice to build strong foundations for all your relationships. Your past provides an opportunity to learn and build a platform for a healthier life in the future.

Close personal relationships are one of the most fulfilling things in life, but, as you know too well, when relationships break down they can also provide one of life's greatest challenges. There are no school lessons on how to make relationships work and, when you think of many of today's politicians, sportspeople, and TV stars, there are few good role models. Is there any hope at all for meaningful relationships?

The answer is a resounding *yes*! Relationships with friends, with family, at work or elsewhere can be strengthened by what you learn from your relationship breakdown.

If you have a willingness to learn and change, you can build the foundations for strong, deep, fulfilling relationships in all areas of your life.

I remember vividly how the baggage that I carried from my divorce initially got in the way of my relationships with friends, family, and work colleagues.

I recall feeling a sense of unease, a lack of confidence, difficulty in making easy conversation: "Do I talk about my divorce?" The self-analysis: "Why are they looking at me in that way? Do they notice my anger?" These were all signs that I had not fully recovered.

I realized that unless I completely worked through the pain and hurt of my relationship breakdown and started to correct my own, less than helpful attitudes, I would take the same problems into my future relationships. Close friends and family generally understood my situation and would make allowances for me, but new friends and work colleagues didn't know, and that made it much, much harder.

Getting rid of the baggage in my life was critical and freed me to enjoy better relationships. I now believe that my experience of relationship breakdown has made all my relationships much stronger and deeper, and I have a number of close friends who have confirmed this to me. I am much more proactive in relationships. I understand myself and my emotions better and am far more able to express myself than I used to be. I am certainly not perfect but I listen more and am far better equipped to resolve problems or arguments. I continue to use these new skills in all my relationships.

What are the key skills that make relationships work?

The interesting fact is that the skills that make a relationship work are the skills that we have already covered in this book. They are:

1. Understanding your emotions and building self-awareness;

2. Being able to communicate by expressing yourself well and listening; and

3. Being able to resolve conflict and let go of the pain that arises.

These three skills are fundamental in any relationship you may have. They are like the mountains of the Himalayas when it comes to the challenge, but the route up them is beautiful and rewarding. They are skills that need to be practised day after day, and the more you develop them, the better your relationships will be.

1. Understanding your feelings and building self-awareness

Understanding your thoughts and feelings, fears and beliefs, motivations and emotions is a core part of building self-awareness. Self-awareness helps you to accelerate healthy change in your life and develop better relationships with other people.

Recognizing your feelings and emotions is the first step in creating healthy change, particularly if they are painful feelings, which can act like landmines waiting to explode in your life. Being aware of these thoughts and feelings enables you to spot and control the emotional triggers or personal traits that may be holding you back. It then empowers you to initiate change in your own life that you can sustain over the long term.

This is what Trisha said:

I had been separated from my husband for about four years and was at a very low point in my life. I felt guilty and blamed myself for the break-up. I got stuck in a revolving door of one relationship after another because I was not healthy inside. It had been emotional turmoil. Initially I didn't want to heal; I just wanted to have a relationship and have a new family. Now I understand that you have to be whole by yourself, rather than get someone to fill a void inside you.

I got married quite young and my husband had become, in a way, my identity. When we divorced I had to find my own identity and that was like a long journey – four years in the valley of despair. But it's been eight years since we separated and I can now say that I am finally starting to build up my confidence.

Understanding my feelings and learning to be self-aware were the main things that helped me. I would have lost much less time if I had concentrated on healing and understanding – it's so important to recognize your feelings, fears, beliefs, and motivations, and I think this is the key to starting to build healthy relationships again. I was very clumsy after my divorce and in a way I had to learn by myself how to be an adult – it meant growing up and it's been good.

Trisha's story, and Robert's earlier, highlight an important point. The more whole you are, the healthier your relationships can be. If you seek a relationship to fill a void inside your heart or purely to make you feel good, then the relationship dynamics will be out of kilter and that will create problems. The more whole and content you are, the easier it is to have balanced, healthy relationships.

This time of huge change in your life becomes a vital phase during which you find out who you are in your own right, rather than who you are as part of a couple. It is an opportunity to seek out what makes you whole and what makes you feel valued.

Spend time reflecting on what is important to you physically, mentally, and spiritually. Read books on the topic and seek out events or courses that will stimulate your thinking in this whole area. Maybe go on a course such as Alpha, a course that looks at the meaning of life. Then, once you know what enables you to feel whole and valued, you can enhance the relationships around you.

Good relationships occur when both parties know what is important to each of them and make a choice to cherish those things. Understanding what makes you feel valued and loved is therefore a key part of understanding what makes a relationship work, be it in the workplace, with your family, or with your friends.

2. Expressing yourself and listening

Understanding our emotions is vital in moving forward successfully and is the first step to expressing ourselves to others. This aspect of communication is critical to building durable relationships with a strong foundation. When combined with good listening skills, it creates a deeper understanding of each other.

It is easy to see that when one person finds it hard to express their thoughts and feelings, or finds it hard to listen, a relationship can suffer. Ultimately, communication is the lifeblood of all relationships. Where there is an easy mix of expressing yourself and listening, healthy relationships can thrive.

3. Resolving conflict and forgiving

A natural consequence of being able to express yourself adequately in any relationship is that differences of opinion will arise and may lead to conflict. Even if the content is fine, it's sometimes the way we say things that leads to arguments!

Rather than not expressing ourselves (for fear of argument), the healthy route is to learn how to resolve the differences that arise. We therefore need to build confidence and practise resolving all types of conflict.

This will deepen relationships, as we become able to raise issues at the same time as respecting and listening to other people's points of view, without the fear of running away.

Vital to this dynamic is an ability to let go of any painful issues that arise during conflict. No one is perfect and all relationships will have aspects that are noted down on the negative side of the relationship scorecard. Forgiveness is a vital skill for letting go of the painful stuff and enabling ongoing relationships to remain healthy.

Personal exercise

Across all your relationships, which of these key tools would you like to develop further?

Robert

I met my ex-wife at a bus station in York when I was twenty-four and she was just turning twenty-two. We fell madly in love and spent three or four years together before we got married. Up to that point everything seemed absolutely perfect. I hate that word now – it was so not perfect.

Shortly after our marriage my stepfather became very unwell and, for the first time ever, I had to lean on my wife.

My stepfather passed away after a few months, so it was really difficult for my family, and that put a huge strain on our relationship.

I am not sure whether it was directly because of that, but she had her first close relationship with someone else within a year of our wedding. It stopped and we decided not to tell anyone, mainly because we wanted to keep it from the family and sort it out ourselves. Although my trust had been smashed, I was still madly in love with her. Because my parents had got divorced when I was six, I was adamant that I was going to get married only once and I vowed I was never going to end up like them.

We tried to work it out and things got a bit better. I remember my thirtieth birthday with her, which was one of the best days of my life. Then slowly she started falling into the same old habits. She stayed longer and longer at work and would sometimes not come back till four in the morning. In the end she told me she was having an affair with a guy at work. The affair seemed to end and I still wanted to reconcile, so again we tried to work it out.

But then after two months she came back to our flat at about two in the morning. I could hear this scraping at the front door and there she was, blind drunk. She said she'd been with the guy again. There was nothing but cold contempt in her face and I felt destroyed in that moment. I'd never seen that look on anyone and that's when life went horribly wrong for me. Luckily a friend arrived before I killed her – I'd never been that angry before.

I moved out for three months, still hoping we could reconcile, and this time, instead of me trying to get her to come back, I was determined that she would have to come to get me. Sadly she never did.

So how did you deal with all the pain?

Well I instantly got into a relationship with someone at work. I was very, very angry and it was all-consuming. It felt like a shield, but in fact it was further wounding me. Then that relationship blew up and I reached a really low point. I was very depressed.

I remember it was 2 January and I was going to work for the first time after the Christmas break and I'd just broken up with another girlfriend. I walked straight past the office, went to the doctor's, and just burst into tears. I couldn't cope any longer with the enormity of what had happened in my life, and I got it all off my chest to the doctor. He gave me a letter to give to my boss, which I had no intention of doing – I'm a proud man and I didn't want any help. I was mentally paralysed, however, and couldn't work. I burst into tears in front of my bosses, which I was pretty ashamed of, but they were amazing.

I was so low I became suicidal. I was in this big block of flats one day and found myself on the roof, and that's when I realized I needed help. I got some antidepressants and they literally saved my life. I had all these wrong preconceptions about antidepressants, but what they did was to help me cope with the situation I was in. They picked me up and I can't recommend them enough – so if you need them, go and get them.

My employers were very understanding and I had six weeks off work. That's when I first came on Restored Lives. On the first night I nearly got thrown out for swearing so much. I was white hot with rage and would just explode at the slightest provocation. It became obvious that this thing was going to kill me if I allowed myself the luxury of hating so much, so forgiveness was a very big turning point for me.

Forgiveness was absolutely impossible at the beginning but, thankfully, during the apocalyptic fall-out, I found out what forgiveness was all about, and that was the real turning point for me. The forgiveness thing wasn't easy, especially as my ex was unwilling to apologize. It was on one of the evenings on the course that I said, "I'm ready to let this go", and that was the start. It wasn't the end of it, by any means, but it was the start of recovery for me.

I got angry again the next day but I said the forgiveness words over and over, and it really did feel as if a weight were lifted off my shoulders. It wasn't a case of, "Well, now I'm free", but I stopped looking back and holding on to all that baggage of hate, anger, resentment, and bitterness – all the things that were basically defining me at the time. I started feeling hope and asking who I really was. Frankly, I'd lost myself and had absolutely no idea who I was. Looking back on it now, it's the best thing that's happened to me. So if there's a message here for anyone struggling with forgiveness, it's this: I know it's a battle and I know you will struggle, but it's essential. There's no getting around it.

It isn't easy even after you've forgiven; it's a continual thing, and it took me about a year of struggling. At first I had to force myself to say, "I wish them well", but it became easier and easier. If you'd told me when I first came on the course that I'd be doing that, I would have laughed in your face, but it has massively transformed me.

This is a good yardstick for how far I've got in my recovery – my best friend got married last August and he gave me the honour of being his best man, while at the same time my ex was chief bridesmaid. I was able to look up the aisle at my ex walking down it and be reminded of our marriage but still have peace in my heart. That was a massive gauge for me of my level of forgiveness and healing. There is hope now.

TOOLBOX TO TAKE AWAY
Building better relationships

Strong relationships help you to focus on the future and give you meaning and purpose

A new intimate relationship is not the solution to your problems

Build strong foundations: when change happens, it gives room for new growth; it's our choice what this will look like

Three skills for making relationships work – like climbing the Himalayas, a massive challenge, but beautiful and rewarding:

1. Understanding your emotions and building self-awareness

- *Self-awareness helps you to accelerate healthy change and develop better relationships.*
- *The more whole you are, the healthier your relationships can be.*
- *Understanding what makes you feel valued is key.*

2. Expressing yourself and listening

- *Essential for building relationships on a lasting basis.*
- *Healthy relationships thrive when there is an easy mix of expressing yourself and listening.*

3. Resolving conflict and forgiving

- *Conflicts and differences of opinion will arise –don't fear them.*
- *Build confidence that you can successfully cope with and resolve all types of conflict.*
- *No one is perfect and all relationships will have aspects that are noted down on the negative side of the relationship.*

- *Forgiveness is a vital skill for keeping ongoing relationships healthy.*

Personal exercise

Across all your relationships, which of these key tools would you like to develop further?

Chapter 12

Restored lives and the next stage

"Your present circumstances don't determine where you go; they merely determine where you start."

Nido Qubein, author and businessman

"Character cannot be developed in ease and quiet. Only through experience of trial and suffering can the soul be strengthened, ambition inspired and success achieved."

Helen Keller, author and political activist (1880–1968)

Each personal story in this book has been included to give you hope that you can get through your relationship breakdown and gain a life free from the effects of the past.

Moreover, our experience is that the tools we have discussed will not only help you get through the break-up of your relationship, but are the same tools that will help you to build strong, meaningful relationships in the future.

I have many other stories of people working through their relationship breakdown who are amazed at the degree of recovery possible in a person's life. Some people have been stuck for many years and only slowly reach a better place. In other cases, I have seen faces change in a matter of weeks –

initially crumpled with pain and tension but soon becoming relaxed, smiling, and content.

The people in this book are normal, everyday people from all walks of life: different backgrounds, different break-ups, different families, different faiths, different levels of income, different hopes, different fears, and different expectations. But they all speak of the same end point – a restored life.

These people are living testimonies to the knowledge that a full recovery can take place and that there *is* life after separation and divorce. You may feel that you are sitting isolated in a small boat in the midst of your own personal storm, but listening to these experiences can become like an ocean liner coming alongside to guide you to a safe harbour.

These people have been through the storm, and here are some of their comments about what recovery is like for them:

"My break-up was like being burned internally in the hell of time. Hurting, doubting, and contemplating the existence of life. Recovery has been like lying in the green pastures, sitting beside still waters. Like a gentle summer breeze caressing the body and slowly but surely healing it back to sanity and splendour. Before, life felt meaningless, and now it is part of a great meaning." Simon

"Recovery is letting go of the pain of the past and looking forward, not back. Remembering the good stuff and trying not to grind on about the bad stuff – 'This will soon pass.' Counting my blessings – even the small ones – as they all add up! Recovery is having great friends and enjoying having a laugh. Recovery is not blaming the past for my future." Cathy

"Recovery can be defined as a healing inside you. It's being ready to move on with your life and ready for new challenges. I would also describe it as forgiveness and acceptance of the situation you have been through." Rosa

"Real recovery began when I no longer identified myself as a divorcee. It's a funny identity to wear, yet it assumes a much bigger role in your life than it deserves. I woke up one day and didn't think about what I had lost. Instead, I began to think about the future in a meaningful way and wonder how it would play out. Divorce had lost its grip on me and life has resumed 'normal service', with all the usual 'ups and downs' that involves." Guy

"Recovery is slow and painful. There are moments when all is well and the children are getting used to our new life. He will always be their father – he chose, or was compelled, to leave us – I am his ex (I find it difficult to say ex-wife). I am well. The children are OK. I am alive, I love, and I am loved. Recovery is that we were involved in something catastrophic and are recovering. We are, and will be, well." Elizabeth

"Recovery is about being able to smile again. It's being able to talk about my marriage without getting upset. It's about accepting the fact that it ended even though it wasn't what I wanted at the time. But now I can look back and think about what was good about my marriage. We have a beautiful daughter, we both love her, and as parents we will try to do our best for her. I'm happy again and that's good!" Debbie

"Recovery is acknowledging that this situation has happened and that I share a joint responsibility for it, in particular responsibility for my own behaviour." Chris

"Recovery is feeling whole again. It is building a new life on your own. Not longing for a relationship but feeling happy with yourself." Arthur

"Recovery is finding myself again and breathing easy. Seeing the colours and hearing the music." Hannah

"Recovery has been a journey on which I have been able to find myself. I feel free to move on and to help others who are struggling. I have learned to accept and forgive, and keep forgiving. I thank God for taking me this far and I know that only he could have turned all the bitter experience around and brought good out of it." George

"Recovery is feeling special and optimistic again. It's waking up happy after sleeping through the night. After years of feeling life was over and hopeless, I now accept the things I cannot change. I don't blame myself; I feel proud to have been kind and honourable and forgive myself for the times I was less than open or totally honest." Louise

"Recovery is an incremental process of rediscovering myself; of realizing I am not a failure or a reject, but a person who has a lot to offer – to my friends, my family, my work colleagues, and even strangers. It is about crawling out of the abyss and starting to live in the moment, noticing the little everyday things that make life worth living: laughter, sudden sunlight, friendly exchanges, or an unexpected hug from one of my children. It is about accepting, learning to forgive, finding that pain dissipates with time, and knowing that even if the future is uncertain, it is survivable, and, on a good day, even exciting." Natalie

Journey of recovery

There is hope of a new and maybe better life. Even though you may neither feel it nor see it at present, there is light at the end of your tunnel. Many people have successfully made this journey and have been through the process of recovery that we saw in Chapter 1:

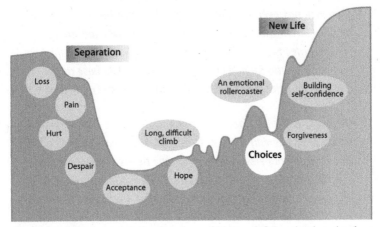

Fix your focus on the final point of "New life", which is higher than the start – it is possible to grow stronger through your relationship breakdown.

Good can come out of painful circumstances. There are many things in life that affirm this:

- a pearl, created when something irritating gets into an oyster;

- the pruning of a rose, when cutting the plant improves its health and lifespan;

- the purification of gold, which has to be refined under intense heat.

It's not something that you can possibly regard as good while it is happening, but, with help and by making the right choices along the way, good will come out of it.

What next?

You will feel different things as you finish this book. There are often three different responses:

"Still stuck"

You may still feel stuck in the same place. You may have just separated, or perhaps you are in the middle of a difficult legal process, or you may still be in shock about your situation. Words such as "I can't seem to move on at all" may characterize your feelings.

If this is you, then try to find some more support during this difficult time. Seek out friends who can listen and help you. Find a counsellor or a divorce course near you – these will help you to work through the problems that you are grappling with. Maybe read again the parts of the book that are most relevant to you and go through the exercises once more.

"I feel fragile but OK"

Others may say, "I feel fragile but OK"; "I'm still working through some things but I can stand on my own two feet now."

If that's how you feel, that's good, but don't get isolated. Recovery consists of a series of ups and downs, so make sure that you keep in touch with people who can help and support you. Continue to be honest about your feelings and ensure that you have an outlet for them.

"I feel reasonably sorted"

Finally, others may say, "I feel OK and reasonably sorted."

If this is you, you are well on your way out of the dark tunnel of relationship breakdown. You are in a strong position to help others on their journey with the tools and experience that you have gained.

There are so many people who go through relationship breakdown without any support. If you can lend a helping hand to just one of them, you can make a huge difference, and it may even help you on your own journey.

My dream is that if each restored person could help two or more people, then we could really start to reduce the impact of relationship breakdown on our society.

Conclusion

Ultimately, there are no easy solutions to the problems and conflicts that arise during and after divorce or separation and we will always have things to learn. Relationships can be seriously challenging, and, equally, they can be the most fulfilling and satisfying part of life.

This book is designed to help you participate fully in meaningful relationships in all areas of your life. Many people who have completed the Restored Lives course wouldn't have believed they could build a new life and yet they have. I want to reassure you that things really can get better; there are good times, friendship, and laughter ahead.

You

The final story is your own.

It's helpful, even healing, to write down your own personal story. It crystallizes in your mind what has happened and where you are on your journey.

Don't worry if your relationship breakdown has just started, or are in the middle of it, but recognize that you are on a journey. Writing a short summary of your story will help you to face up to what you are still feeling and will give you a record that you can look back at in the future – even if it is only a short list of bullet points, it's a helpful process.

I have included a suggested structure below, but you don't have to fill in every area. Write down the major milestones and significant choices or the tipping points in your life, particularly those moments relating to acceptance and forgiveness, and include any future steps that you now want to take or goals that you have.

It started when:

The most painful times were when:

The major issues were:

The major milestones were:

I can now accept that:

I have forgiven:

I want to move on by:

My goal is to:

Show someone your story or email it to me through our website (www.restoredlives.org) – these stories are important and precious.

THE SUMMARY TOOLBOX

1. Recognizing and dealing with your emotions

- *Recognizing your emotions, and owning them, is a vital start of the process of moving on.*
- *If these emotions are painful, then pain needs a response. It's no good just leaving them, like landmines ready to explode sometime in the future.*

- *We looked at some ways of surviving each day, such as noticing the moment; living one day at a time; laughing and being kind to yourself.*
- *We banned the thought that "I am a failure". One relationship has failed. You are not a failure. You have other successful relationships, gifts, talents, and skills, and a bright future ahead of you.*
- *We discussed some of the ways of dealing with longer-term feelings such as anger, fear, and depression.*

2. Building confidence through communicating and resolving conflict

- *A better ability to communicate with your ex is a vital tool that builds your self-confidence.*
- *The important points here are a positive personal attitude – "We can't change our ex but we can change our own attitude for the better."*
- *Being able to express yourself.*
- *Being able to listen to a person and reflect back to them what they said.*
- *Creating healthy boundaries.*
- *Not fearing conflict – with the tools for resolving conflict you can deal with these difficult situations.*

3. Letting go of the past

- *Acceptance is important.*
- *Forgiveness is the key tool for letting go.*
- *Forgiveness means:*
  - *choosing to release someone from punishment;*
  - *ceasing to hold it against them.*

- *Doing this every time those painful memories come back to haunt you is a vital process.*
- *All this together gives you freedom and enables you to let go of all the baggage.*

4. Building successful relationships

You are going through a huge change in your life and this has an impact on your children, family, friends, and social circles. To cope with these changes it's helpful to:

- *Have a trusted friend to come alongside you.*
- *Try not to worry when friendships change – it's part of the process.*
- *Start to look for new activities, to find new friends and interests.*
- *On the topic of children, look at being able to listen and respond to your children.*
- *Agree new ways of parenting together with your ex, using a letter to set out new goals and guidelines.*

All these tools will help to boost your confidence and give you a renewed belief that close and enriching personal relationships are most certainly still possible.

Restored Lives
– THE COURSE

If you would like to know details about the Restored Lives course, or read further stories and comments, there is more information on our website: www.restoredlives.org

If you are interested in running a course, the website has details of how to get started and there is now a course DVD and accompanying workbook available from Monarch:

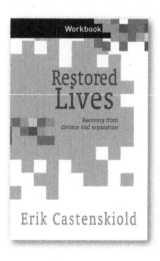 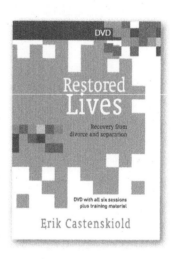

The Restored Lives range:

main book	978-0-85721-476-8
seven session DVD with full presentations	978-0-85721-479-9
40-page workbook	
single copies:	978-0-85721-478-2
packs of ten:	978-0-85721-477-5